BEAT
THE BANK

Paul Meredith

BEAT THE BANK

HOW TO WIN
THE MORTGAGE GAME IN CANADA

PAUL MEREDITH

SeaLord Publishing

SeaLord Publishing
2104 Yonge St.,
Toronto, ON M4S 2A5

10 9 8 7 6 5 4 3 2 1
Library and Archives Canada Cataloguing in Publication

Meredith, Paul J., 1971-, author
   Beat the bank : how to win the mortgage game in Canada / Paul Meredith.

ISBN 978-0-9938551-3-9 (softcover)

   1. **Mortgage loans--Canada. 2. Housing--Finance.**
I. Title.

   HG2040.5.C2M47 2017   332.7'220971   C2017-901843-4

Quantity sales. Special discounts are available on quantity purchases by corporations, associations, and others. For details, contact the author directly at paulm@citycan.com

Paul Meredith, Mortgage Broker, CityCan Financial Corp. Lic. 10532
paulm@citycan.com   www.easy123mortgage.ca

Table of Contents

ACKNOWLEDGEMENTS

MAKING THE DECISION TO WRITE a book can be an overwhelming experience, let alone the process of actually writing it. It's taken over two years to complete, with many interuptions and setbacks during the process. With perseverance, dedication and commitment, I was able to see it through to completion. This book was originally slated for release in the fall of 2016, and the final draft was completed by late September of that year. Almost as if on queue, new mortgage regulations were announced days later that required me to go through, change and re-write certain pieces of content throughout the book. Everything needed to be accurate and fully up to date for its release. Just one more hurdle I needed to overcome. No problem at all!

There are several people I would like to thank who helped make Beat the Bank the fine piece of Canadian literature that it is. What? Too dramatic?

I would first like to thank my very good friend Peter Kelly, for the many hours spent going through every page meticulously. This was a very busy and challenging time for him in his life, both personally and professionally. The fact that he took so much time out of his crazy schedule to proof read, edit and offer suggestions means a lot to me. His input has lead to better and more polished final version.

Next I'd like to thank my wonderful and amazing mom. Going through line by line and picking out every single word, letter and typo that were missed from previous edits is a chore in itself. Just when I thought I had caught all the typos, she of course finds more.

Thank you so much for taking the time mom! You're the greatest mom in the world and I love you very much!

And then there is Shayne Slinn. While I'm confident in my math, I'm very grateful to have Shayne's math wizardry at my fingertips to verify all my calculations and correct any mathematical typos. He played an important role and his input was very much appreciated.

I of course can't forget about my beautiful girlfriend Kelly who encouraged and pushed me throughout the entire process. She also played a significant role in the final editing of the book. She's a very important person in my life and she is always there for me in every way possible. I love you baby, you mean everything to me!

INTRODUCTION

I CAN STILL REMEMBER WHEN I applied for my first mortgage. I had recently been through some serious financial turmoil after making some bad business decisions. My level of debt had become significant, and my income was fairly low. Despite my troubles, I was tired of paying rent and really wanted to buy a place of my own now that I was earning a regular salary, although not a lot.

The thought of looking for a mortgage both excited and scared me. I had struggled with credit issues and business failures in my 20's, and I felt I was just now starting to get a handle on everything.

I walked into one of the major banks to see if I could get approved for a mortgage. As I was still rebuilding my credit and my income was fairly low, I knew it probably wasn't possible for me. But hey, I had nothing to lose by trying! So I walked in, met with a mortgage advisor (let's call her Sandra).... and applied. She didn't give me very much information and said she would get back to me.

A couple of days later, she called and told me I was approved for $320,000.

I was ecstatic!

I couldn't believe they approved me. I was so happy!

Then the logical side of my brain kicked in. I realized they didn't check my credit, nor did they even ask me about my debt, which was still quite high in relation to my income. In fact, it was double my annual income!

"How can they approve me for anything without even checking my credit or asking about my debt?", I thought.

I questioned this and Sandra told me to just go shopping for a home up to the 'pre-approved' value and then come back to them when I found something. They said that they would be reviewing my debt and credit at that time.

What?

I knew absolutely nothing about mortgages, but it just didn't seem right to me. I told them that I didn't want to waste my time if I wasn't going to be approved. She then reluctantly took down the rest of my information so she could proceed with a credit check and she told me it would be a couple of days (as an experienced broker now, I still wonder what could have possibly taken so long).

A few days later, I followed up with Sandra as I had not yet heard from her (or from anyone else at the bank for that matter). When I called her extension, someone else answered, so I of course asked for Sandra.

The response I got was an ecstatic... "Did you hear the good news???" I asked if the good news was that I was approved. After finding out who I was, she said, oh.. no. You have been declined, but Sandra was promoted...isn't that great?!?!"

Seriously????

There was silence for what seemed like thirty seconds, but in reality was probably only five. I couldn't believe what I was hearing.

Needless to say, as great as the news was that Sandra was promoted, there couldn't have been anything I could have cared less about at that particular time.

I had more questions and was once again told they would have to get back to me. Unfortunately, nobody ever did.

Every time I thought about mortgages, I would think back to that experience. It shouldn't have been that challenging to find out something as simple as whether I was approved for a mortgage or not. People should be able to find out if they qualify quickly, and they need to be treated with more respect. They shouldn't have to wait days to have their questions answered.

Since I wasn't happy with my current profession, I decided to look at a career in mortgages.

MY VENTURE INTO THE MORTGAGE WORLD

When I started in this business, I wanted to ensure that my clients had a better experience than I did. I always think back how to unimportant I was made to feel and strive to treat all my clients with respect and appreciation. I believe everyone deserves to have their questions answered quickly and professionally and should never be left in the dark, wondering if anything is actually being done. Communication is crucial to their overall experience, so communication they will get!

I've based my business on providing this level of service to my clients and have always said… "I'll always be there for you when you need me." Everyone deserves better treatment than what I went through. I have never strayed from this mentality.

Having worked as a mortgage broker since 2007, I have noticed many patterns among mortgage seekers that they may not be aware of. These negative patterns are costing them literally thousands of their hard earned dollars, while padding the massive profits of the banks.

I make every effort to steer my clients in the right direction and take the time to help them understand their options. I give my clients the same advice as I would give my own family. And to me, my clients are like family.

I wrote this book to help more people gain clarity on the mortgage industry, learn how the various professionals work, and what to look out for on their mortgages. Much of the advice contained in this book is not something that your local mortgage banker will provide, and in some cases, it's advice they don't want you to get.

Why would I share this hard earned knowledge?

Helping other people is something that gives me a tremendous amount of happiness. The more people I feel I'm helping, the happier I become. I'm smiling right now as I'm writing this.

Not everyone out there is as honest as they could be. It's unfortunate that some are just in it to make a quick buck for themselves with no concern for the well being of the client. These kinds of tactics sicken me, and they hurt the industry as a whole. This is why it is so important to ask questions before hiring a mortgage professional, regardless of whether it is a broker or the mortgage specialist at a bank.

Banks, like any other business, are there for one reason, and that is to make a profit. There is definitely nothing wrong with that, but banks have certain policies that you may not be aware of that can end up costing you thousands of dollars. If you aren't aware of what is going on, you may fall right into their trap. By providing clarity on what you should be looking for, you can get closer to paying off that mortgage all that much quicker. You can be the one with the last laugh by 'beating the bank' at their own game.

How to use this book

There are exceptions to every rule and not every suggestion made in this book will be right 100% of the time. This information will give you an idea of what you should be looking out for when shopping for a mortgage to help ensure you're being treated fairly.

There are parts of this book that are written for the first time home buyer, while other parts are for more experienced mortgage shoppers. This book does not need to be read cover to cover. Instead, I suggest skipping straight to the sections that are of most interest to you.

Not everything will be applicable in every situation. In some cases I'll be generalizing to appeal to the most amount of people. The information provided is a combination of facts and personal opinion based on my ten years of experience as a mortgage broker. Individual situations may vary, so I recommend seeking professional advice based on your specific needs.

When speaking about individuals, I'll be using the word 'he', as opposed to 'he or she' in order to keep everything simple. For the purposes of this book, 'he' is to be interpreted as a gender-neutral term.

In certain examples, I'll be using fictitious names to illustrate certain points. Anyone actually having these names would be purely coincidental.

It's now time to get started in giving you the upper hand so you can Beat the Bank at their own game!

CHAPTER ONE

MORTGAGES 101

FOR A FIRST TIME HOMEBUYER, there is no question that shopping for a mortgage can be somewhat overwhelming. Fixed, variable, open, closed, amortization, shorter terms, longer terms, HELOCs, high-ratio, conventional, etc., etc. The list of common terminology goes on and on. There are literally hundreds of combinations and there is no question it can be enough to make your head spin if you're new to the mortgage world.

So how do you determine which mortgage is right for you?

It starts with having an understanding of what each of these options actually mean, which will make it easier for you to make an informed decision.

If you're new to the exciting world of mortgages (okay, maybe not that exciting), then there is some common terminology you'll need to become familiar with which will be repeated throughout this book.

Term

This is the amount of time your mortgage contract with the lender is valid for. The most common term length is 5 years, but terms can be as short as 6 months, or as long as 10 years…and everything in between. At the end of your term, your contract with your mortgage lender expires and balance becomes due and payable. At this point you have three options:

1. Pay the mortgage off in full if you happen to have won the lottery.
2. Renew your mortgage with your current lender at a new term of your choice. The rate provided will be rate offered by that particular lender at that time.
3. Switch your mortgage over to another lender, which gives you the ability to shop around.

I'll be explaining more about these options in Chapter Seven.

Amortization

This is the amount of time it would take for you to pay your mortgage down to a zero balance assuming equal payments. The most common amortization is 25 years, however with a down payment or equity position of 20% or more, you can go as high as 30 years. With new mortgage regulations announced back in October 2016, options with 30 year amortization are more limited than they were in previous years, however they still are readily available.

Loan to Value (LTV)

Loan to value is the amount of your mortgage in relation to the value of the property expressed as a percentage. For example, if you were to purchase a home with a down payment of 5%, the LTV is 95%. If you had a 20%, the LTV would be 80%. If zero down was still possible, it would be 100% LTV.

Fixed Rate Mortgage

As the name implies, a fixed rate mortgage is where both your rate and your payment are fixed for the mortgage term. Regardless of what the market does or where interest rates move, your rate and payment will remain the same. A fixed rate mortgage is suited to borrowers who are less tolerant to risk and feel more comfortable knowing that their payment is fixed for the entire term. Fixed rate mortgages are *almost* always higher than variable rate mortgages.

Variable Rate / Adjustable Rate Mortgage

Unlike a fixed rate, your rate and payment will fluctuate with prime rate on variable rate mortgages. Prime rate is set by the Bank of Canada, who typically has seven scheduled rate announcements per year. Unscheduled rate announcements are possible, but quite rare. When the prime rate changes, so does your rate, and most commonly, so does your payment. I'll be talking more about variable rates later in the chapter.

Home Equity Line of Credit

The Home Equity Line of Credit, most often referred to as a HELOC, is the most common form of open mortgage. You could have your entire mortgage in a HELOC if you like, which can go up to a maximum 65% loan to value (see above for LTV definition). As a HELOC works just like any other line of credit, you can pay as much towards it as you choose, or can pay as little as just the interest owing for the month. You can also re-access the money back up to the credit limit whenever you need it.

Sounds great, right?

Why doesn't everyone have a HELOC then? They likely would if it wasn't for the higher interest rate that they carry. While lower than a typical open mortgage, it's still quite a bit higher than that of closed mortgages. At the time of writing, the rate on a HELOC is approximately one percent higher than the current variable rate.

Most people of course won't want to have their entire mortgage in a HELOC simply because of the comparatively high interest rate. There is an option however that will allow you to split your mortgage into two components. One being an amortized loan (mortgage), which would represent the bulk of the money owed. The other being a HELOC, for a much smaller portion, or even a zero balance to start off. This type of set up will allow you to go up to 80% of the property's value (LTV) as long as the HELOC portion does not exceed 65% LTV. This would be referred to as a multi-component, or 'hybrid' mortgage.

COMMONLY MISUNDERSTOOD TERMS

High Ratio Vs. Conventional Mortgages

All mortgages are placed into one of two categories, high ratio or conventional, depending on the amount of your down payment. If your down payment is 20% or greater, your mortgage is classified as conventional. If it's less than 20%, it would be considered high-ratio.

Any high-ratio mortgage will require mortgage default insurance, which is simply insurance protecting the lender in the event of default by the borrower. In other words, if you think it might be more fun to shoot off to Vegas for the weekend than it would be to make your mortgage payment, you would then be considered in default. Not that Vegas isn't fun!

The cost of the mortgage default insurance varies depending on the amount of your down payment. The premium is paid by the borrower and added to the mortgage amount.

For example, with a 5% down payment, the mortgage default insurance is 4.00% of the mortgage amount compared with 3.10% with 10% down and 2.80% with 15% down. The greater your down payment, the lower your insurance premium.

At present, there are three companies offering mortgage default insurance, which are CMHC, Genworth and Canada Guaranty. CMHC is the most widely recognized of the three, so mortgage default insurance is commonly referred to by many as CMHC insurance.

While the purpose of mortgage default insurance is to serve the lender, it's not as though the borrower doesn't get anything out of it. It allows people to purchase a home with as little as 5% down.

Without it, 20% would be the minimum requirement, which would put home ownership out of reach for many.

I'll be talking more about down payment in Chapter Six.

Variable Rate vs. Adjustable Rate Mortgages

You'll often hear floating rate mortgages referred to as either variable or adjustable rate mortgages (ARM). The terms ARM and Variable Rate Mortgage, or simply 'variable', are often used interchangeably by both consumers and industry professionals alike. However, there is a difference between the two if you want to go by strict definition.

With both types, the interest rate changes with the prime rate. If the prime rate moves up or down by 0.25%, then so does your interest rate. Where they differ is the payment amount. With a true variable, when your rate changes, your payment still remains the same. The increase or decrease in interest paid is reflected in the amortization. If the rate drops, your amortization will automatically drop (the date in which your mortgage becomes paid off in full would be sooner). Since your payment remains the same, more of the payment would then go to principal, which in turn reduces the amortization. If the rate increases, then more of the payment goes to interest and less to principal, therefore increasing your amortization.

With ARMs, the payment changes along with the interest rate. True variable rate mortgages are almost non-existent these days and almost everything available is an ARM. As the term 'variable' is the popular term for all floating rate mortgages, I'll be referring to it as a variable throughout the book to keep in line with common and familiar terminology.

Open vs. Closed

A mortgage is considered open or closed based on its terms of prepayment. An open mortgage allows you to pay off the entire mortgage at any time during the term without incurring a penalty. Very similar to the payment terms of a credit card or line of credit in this sense, however you would not be able to re-access the funds once it's been paid. Open mortgages are actually quite rare, and for the most part, they don't make sense as they carry a much higher interest rate. They are meant to be short term solutions only, which is why the maximum term offered on an open mortgage is usually 6 months.

Most mortgages are closed, meaning that terms of prepayment are limited and paying the mortgage off in full will incur a penalty. I'll be talking more about penalties for breaking your mortgage in Chapter Seven.

Hybrid Mortgages

Still can't decide between fixed and variable?

Some lenders offer multi component mortgages which would allow you to take a portion as fixed and a portion as variable. The portion size of each is up to you. It could be 50/50, or it could be 90/10. You can also throw in a HELOC as well and make it three components. Or even more if you wanted to get into adding components with varying terms as well. With some banks, you can have as many as 99 different components, however this would be a nightmare for anyone to follow!

Why anyone would add in varying terms is beyond me, but they do from time to time. A big problem with these hybrid mortgages containing components of varying terms is that it locks you into that bank. If you have a 2 year term and a 5 year term as part of the same mortgage, you can't move the 2 year term to another bank as there is still three years remaining on the other portion. The only way is to break it and pay the penalty.

Even if you keep all terms equal, all multi-component mortgages are registered as collateral mortgages.

How does this affect you? Glad you asked!

With most traditional mortgages, you are free to switch your mortgage to another lender at the end of your term at no cost to you. There is a cost involved, but the new lender will typically pick up that cost making it appear as though it is 'free'. With a collateral mortgage, it has to be discharged at the end of the term if you are going to switch it to another lender. This means that you have to pay the discharge fee, legal fee, and possible appraisal fee if you want to change. This gives you less negotiating power at time of renewal, as the bank knows full well it will cost you if you want to leave them. I'll be talking more about collateral mortgages in Chapter Seven.

Most lenders do not offer HELOCs or hybrid mortgages, so you'll be fairly limited to the big banks, credit unions, and possibly one or two monoline (non-bank) lenders. For that reason, you may not get as low a rate on the mortgage portion as what might be possible elsewhere.

THE NEW AGE OF MORTGAGES

On October 3rd, 2016, Canadian Finance Minister Bill Morneau announced new mortgage regulations in attempt to cool a very hot housing market. As a result, many will now find it much harder to qualify for a mortgage and quoting rates has become more complicated than it really needs to be.

As a result of these changes, most lenders are classifying mortgages into two categories:

Insurable and uninsurable.

INSURABLE

Most mortgages by non-bank lenders and some mortgages from the big banks are 'bulk insured'. In other words, CMHC (for example) is insuring these mortgages on the back end. This allows the lender to securitize them, which is taking an illiquid mortgage loan and converting it into a tradable security (I'll be talking more about this in Chapter Three).

If your down payment is 20% or greater, the insurance premium is paid by the lender. This is nothing new as lenders have been doing this for decades. What is new is the additional limitations that have led to a new category of conventional mortgages called *insurable*.

These limitations on insurable mortgages are as follows:

- 25 year maximum amortization
- Maximum purchase price must be less than $1 million.
- Qualification is based on the benchmark rate set by the Bank of Canada, which is typically much higher than your contract rate (the rate your payments are based on).

UN-INSURABLE

Anything outside of the above limits would be considered un-insurable, which would allow for the following:

- 30 year amortization
- Purchase price over $1 million
- Qualification based on contract rate. This applies to 5 year fixed only. Shorter terms and variable still need to qualify based on the benchmark rate, which is nothing new.

Any existing mortgage being refinanced is also considered uninsurable, regardless of whether it fits within the parameters of an insurable mortgage or not.

The minimum down payment is 20% or greater for all uninsurable mortgages. Any mortgage with less than 20% down would fall under the category of insurable.

The best mortgage rates will typically be with insurable mortgages since the lenders are able to securitize these loans. As this is no longer an option for them on uninsurable mortgages, there is an increase to the cost of funds as they now have to find alternate sources of funding.

The result?

Higher rates. The cost of an uninsurable mortgage can be as much as 25 basis points (0.25%) higher than that of an insurable mortgage, or even higher. I've seen the difference as high as 50 basis points.

PRE-APPROVAL

Now that you have a good understanding of the basic mortgage lingo, it's time to get serious. It doesn't matter if you are a first time homebuyer or if you've been buying and selling homes for years. Before you begin shopping for a new home, you'll want to get pre-approved to find out how much you'll qualify for.
Never assume you will qualify for a mortgage!

While you may think you have solid credit, a credit bureau can sometimes contain 'surprises'. That is, possible collections or delinquencies that you may not be aware of. They can be legitimate or erroneous, but either way you'll want to ensure your credit is solid before proceeding with home shopping. The last thing you want is to get all excited about finding your dream home only to find out that you don't qualify due to a 'glitch' with your credit.

A credit bureau can sometimes contain possible collections or delinquencies that you may not be aware of

A preapproval will also tell you how much you'll qualify for. I see time and time again, people trying to purchase homes that are out of their qualified price range.

Most realtors will also expect you to have a preapproval before they will take you out to look at listings. They want to ensure you'll actually qualify for the homes they're showing you, not to mention, a preapproved client is more attractive to a seller than one is not.

Most real estate purchase agreements automatically give you five business days to obtain financing satisfactory to you. However, in situations where the housing market is particularly hot, you may need to waive the finance condition if you want to have a chance at landing your dream home. This is where a preapproval is crucial. Before any broker or bank agrees to let you put in an offer without a finance condition, they should verify all your documentation to ensure everything is in line before giving you the green light. You may think your situation is solid, but the world of mortgage financing can be complex and confusing. Not to mention, it sometimes even defies what is seemingly common sense.

Some of the snags that could create issues with your approval are as follows:

- Probationary employment
- Non-permanent employment
- Insufficient employment history
- Self-employed status
- Insufficient or unacceptable down payment
- Thin credit (not enough credit)
- Past or current credit delinquencies that you may or may not be aware of
- Outstanding collections that you may or may not be aware of

The above are some of the more common situations, however the list can go on and on. The point is… make sure you get preapproved!

CHAPTER ONE HIGHLIGHTS

- Understand the basic terminology before shopping for a mortgage.
- Mortgages fall into two main categories: Insurable and Uninsurable.
- A better rate can often be given on an insurable mortgage.
- Get a pre-approval.
- Never make an assumption that you will qualify for a mortgage.

Having a decent understanding of the basics can eliminate some of the mind-clutter when talking to a professional about getting your first mortgage. You want to be focused more on the options that are open to you, rather than just trying to get a handle on the basics. This alone will help to give you a better experience with your mortgage and focus on the task at hand... selecting the right mortgage for you, which is what we'll be discussing next.

CHAPTER TWO

CHOOSING THE RIGHT MORTGAGE FOR YOU

W ITH SO MANY CHOICES AVAILABLE to you, mortgage shopping can be somewhat overwhelming, even for the experienced mortgage shopper. I have potential clients contacting me regularly saying that they would like to go with a variable rate or a mortgage with a specific term. I'll often ask why they would like to go with that specific product. One of the most common answers I get is that this is what they have always done and that it's worked out well for them in the past. In many cases, it may have been the first product that was sold to them when they got their first mortgage and have stuck with it ever since.

But is it really what's best for them every time their mortgage comes up for renewal?

SELECTING THE RIGHT TERM

When you walk into a bank looking for a mortgage, the first rate they quote you is a 5 year fixed or a 5 year variable. These terms have become standard, but who was it that all of a sudden decided that the 5 year mortgage is the best choice for everyone?

Many mortgage agents will often do the same thing. They quote their clients a 5 year rate without ever taking the time to even consider that this might not be the best option for them.

For example, if Bill and Jane just purchased a new condo, but are planning on starting a family, then it is very unlikely they will still be in that condo in five years time. The chances of breaking their mortgage before the end of the term are strong. In a year or two, they may be looking to upgrade to something that better suits their needs. Sure, they could end up porting their mortgage, which I will discuss later, but this isn't always the best option for people either. The mortgage professional should present a 1 or 2 year option, and then explain the benefits of the shorter term.

Any situation where your future is uncertain would make you an ideal candidate for a mortgage with a shorter term. After all, who's to say you aren't going to meet your dream man or woman the day after closing and get married a year later? (Assuming you're single of course!) There are many reasons that could prevent you from making it to the end of your term.

So why do people feel so comfortable with the 5 year fixed?

We have been conditioned by the banks to think the 5 year fixed is what we need, so we sign the mortgage documents without giving it a second thought.

After all, the mortgage specialist has your best interests in mind, right?

In some cases, they very well may, but you definitely can't rely on that. You need to protect yourself by having a good understanding of your own situation rather than just relying on the mortgage specialist's advice.

In most cases, both banks and mortgage brokers alike will make more money selling 5 year terms over shorter terms, so often this is what they try to sell you. Don't get me wrong here, there are many situations where a 5 year fixed IS the right mortgage for someone, but that's not always the case. Many people feel comfortable knowing that their rate and payment will remain the same for the next five years, which is one of the reasons why five year fixed terms are so popular. However, many people still end up breaking their mortgage before the end of 5 years. In many cases, it's quite likely the term of their mortgage wasn't even discussed at time of application and the only option presented was 5 years. This is doing the customer a disservice as who's to say the 5 year mortgage was right for them in the first place? After all, if a 5 year term was right for everyone, then why are so many homeowners breaking it early? Hmmmm.

All that being said, the 5 year fixed has become the 'standard', however that doesn't mean it's for everyone. Far from it.

A five year mortgage term is not right for everyone.

Take the time to research your options and have a clear understanding of your needs and goals. This will help to ensure you are being offered a mortgage that is right for you rather than just relying on the advice of the mortgage specialist.

In some cases, the 5 year fixed may however be the only option you'll qualify for. Terms shorter than 5 years and variable rate mortgages have to qualify based on the 5 year 'benchmark' rate, which is substantially higher. Some 5 year fixed mortgages qualify based on the contract rate (the rate your payments are based on). This means you can qualify for a higher mortgage amount by choosing a 5 year fixed term, and in some cases, it may be the only option you'll qualify for.

This qualifying difference applies only to uninsurable[1], conventional mortgages. That is, mortgages with at least 20% down payment or 20% equity position (if refinancing). For purchases with less than 20% down, all mortgages have to qualify based on the benchmark rate, regardless of term.

THE 10 YEAR FIXED MORTGAGE TERM

In recent years, the 10 year fixed term has started to become popular as it gives homeowners an opportunity to lock in a low rate for a longer period. This is a product that many banks and mortgage agents alike have been suggesting for their clients. The argument being that rates are going way up and they need to lock in a rate to protect themselves. It needs to be mentioned that both mortgage agents and banks make more money on 10 year mortgages than they do on shorter terms, so they have a vested interest in pushing them. You need to be cautious here.

With rates being near historical lows at the time of writing, there is definitely more room for them to move upward than downward. However, ten years is a long time to lock into any single mortgage term considering that many borrowers don't even make it to the end of their five year term, yet alone make it to the end of a ten year.

---

1   For the differences between insurable and uninsurable, refer to The New Age of Mortgages in Chapter One.

Ask yourself this….

Have you ever lived in one home for longer than ten years?

While some have, most move around far more frequently than that.

Does that mean that 10 year fixed terms should be avoided?

I couldn't in good conscious come out and say yes without knowing more about you. What I can say is you need to ask yourself some serious questions and fully understand what you are getting into before making that decision. I do however think that ten year fixed terms are not the right choice for most people.

Why?

It's because nobody expects to break their mortgage mid-term, but it happens all the time, and sometimes we are forced to. You never know when life will throw you a curveball. I have seen multiple clients with perfect credit and financial stability come back to me a couple of years later with their credit and financial situation in shambles. Sometimes bad things happen to good people and life doesn't always go as we would like it to.

Here are some reasons why some people may end up breaking their mortgage before the end of ten years, many of which are less than pleasant:

- Loss of job
- Transfer of job
- Personal injury or disability
- Illness requiring expensive medication
- Divorce
- Death of spouse
- Relocating out of province or country
- Finances get out of control and need to refinance
- Raise cash to start a business, education, renovations, etc.
- You're self-employed and business takes a turn for the worst

A 10 year fixed mortgage typically carries a rate of around one percent higher the 5 year fixed. You would need to make it right to the end of the 10 year term for it to even have a chance at working out for you. Let me take a moment to break the numbers down so you can see for yourself how everything looks on paper.

Let's say we have two options:

A 5 year fixed at 4.00% and a 10 year fixed at 5.00%

Your mortgage amount is $300,000 and you are amortizing over 25 years with monthly payments.

At the end of five years, your ending balance on the 10 year term will be $265,522.87 compared with only $250,115.61 on the 5 year term. This means that at the five year mark, you'll be ahead by $15,407.26[1] with a 5 year fixed over the 10 year alternative. If you were to break your mortgage at this point, this is the amount of money it would have cost you unnecessarily if you originally selected the 10 year term. This doesn't even include the penalty to break your mortgage, which would add on thousands more.[2]

That covers the first 5 years. Now we have to consider what the rate would be at renewal if you went with the 5 year term. This is of course an unknown variable and all we can do is speculate.

Using the information we have available to us now, we can calculate the break-even rate, which in this case would be 6.50%.

This means that the rate for the remaining 5 years (to round out the 10 years) would have had to be higher than 6.50% for the 10 year mortgage to have made sense. Providing of course that you can even make it all the way to the end of the 10 year term. If the 5 year rate turns out to be lower than 6.50%, then

---

1   Savings is always calculated by using the payment from the higher rate for both options and then calculating the difference between the ending balance for each

2   If breaking a longer term mortgage after 5 years, the penalty is always three months interest.

you would have been better off with the 5 year term from the get go.

One thing that we can all agree on is that 10 years is a long time. Think about where you were 10 years ago. Here are some questions you can ask yourself to help put it into perspective;

What movies were out at that time?
What was the number one hit song?
Where were you living?
Where were you working?
What was your relationship status?
How old were your kids?

I've had clients come to me wanting to break their 10 year fixed mortgage as early as one year into the term. When they originally signed for it, they too thought they would be in it for the long haul. Using the above example, taking a 10 year fixed term is commensurate with betting $15,407.26 that mortgage rates will be higher than 6.50% in 5 years time.

Is that a bet you are willing to take?

THE AGE OLD QUESTION -FIXED OR VARIABLE?

In the past, homeowners have typically come out ahead with variable rate mortgages over fixed. For this reason alone, many of them continue to follow that trend. However, after the 2007-2008 housing collapse in the United States, the variable rate options went from having discounts off prime rate to premiums on top of prime. Before the collapse, the going variable rate was prime-0.60% to prime-0.90%. Then variable rates started to increase, and increase fast. It wasn't long before we were looking at rates anywhere from prime +0.60% to prime +1%, making variable rate mortgages equal to or even higher than fixed rates. The shocking part is that I had clients come to me who were actually locked into these higher rates.

Why would someone go with a variable rate mortgage if they can get a fixed mortgage at a lower rate?

Since the variable rate mortgage had always worked for them in the past, this is what they would go into their bank asking for. Without the mortgage specialist taking the time to properly explain why variable rate mortgages were no longer the better way to go, people would sign for them based on past performance.

Variable rate mortgages started to settle back down shortly thereafter and for a while, the fixed and variable were right around the same rate. With a variable rate mortgage, there is always a risk of the rate increasing during the term vs. no risk of a fixed rate increasing.

So why take a risk if the rate is the same?

The past does not equal the future, especially in this case. In the past when people came out ahead with a variable rate, the discount off prime was often greater than one percent when compared with the 5 year fixed. The larger the spread between fixed and variable rates, the less risky the variable option becomes. The smaller the spread, the more risky.

In more recent years, people have still come out ahead with variable based on much thinner spreads. From September 2010 until early 2017 (the time of writing), there wasn't a single increase to prime rate. This represents one of the longest streaks in history without seeing an increase. Given this rare occurrence, going variable with a thin spread.... sometimes as little as 0.05%, can be a risk that is too much to bare. Taking a variable rate in this case is no different than gambling.

The larger the spread between fixed and variable rates, the less risky the variable option becomes. The smaller the spread, the more risky.

IS VARIABLE RIGHT FOR YOU?

When choosing between fixed and variable, one borrower may not feel comfortable with any sort of risk at all while another may have a very high risk threshold. Your choice really comes down to where on the spectrum you fall, and your mortgage professional should take the time to discuss this with you. Sometimes I'll suggest for a client to go fixed, but then I may suggest variable to the very next client I speak with. Just because a specific mortgage is right for one person doesn't mean it's right for another. If you aren't comfortable with the fact that your rate and payment could increase at any time, then a variable rate mortgage probably isn't for you, regardless of how big the spread is.

There is one additional benefit to variable over fixed. If you found yourself in a position where you needed to break your mortgage early, then the penalty may be lower… in some cases, substantially lower. I'll be talking about penalties in depth in Chapter Seven.

SHORT TERM VS. VARIABLE

In some cases, a mortgage with a shorter term can make more sense than a variable. Shorter term fixed mortgages typically have lower rates than the 5 year fixed, which would narrow the spread over variable. Whenever considering a variable rate mortgage, you may want to consider shorter fixed terms as well. While not always the case, the mortgage rate on a 2 year term could be as much as half a percent (or even more) lower than the 5 year fixed. This can result in a fair amount of savings over the length of the shorter term.

For example, on a $300,000 mortgage with a 25 year amortization and a 5 year fixed rate of 2.99%, the balance after 3 years would be $274,604.95 .

Now let's compare this with a 3 year fixed term at 2.49% where the balance would only be $270,175.76[1] at the end of the term. A difference of $4,429.19.

After 3 years, the break even rate would be 3.86%, meaning that the 2 year fixed (to round out the 5 years) would have to be higher than 3.86% for you to have come out ahead with the 5 year fixed option. If the 2 year fixed was lower than 3.86% at the end of 3 years, then the 3 year term would have been the better choice.

This same strategy can be used with other combinations as well. You can take all 1 year terms, two 2's and a 1 year term….. or any combination you feel comfortable with.

---

1   When calculating savings on one rate vs. another, the payments need to be made equal to that of the higher rate. The difference between the balance at the end of the two year period for each option will be the savings. By making the payments the same, it compensates for the time value of money, which is the most accurate way to calculate mortgage rate savings.

SELECTING YOUR AMORTIZATION

Ever since the Canadian Finance Minister reduced the maximum amortization from 40 years all the way down to 25 years for all high-ratio mortgages (less than 20% down payment) or 30 years for uninsurable, conventional mortgages (20% or more down payment/equity), the decision becomes a whole lot easier. So do you go with 25 years? 30 years? Or cut it down to 20 years?

The answer to this really depends on your particular situation and comfort levels, not to mention what you can afford. Amortization is simply the amount of time it takes to pay your balance down to zero, assuming equal payments. It is not carved in stone and can always be lowered simply by increasing your payments, or by taking advantage of lump sum prepayment options. So keep that in mind when selecting your amortization.

For example, if you select a 30 year amortization but then set your payments as though it were 25 years, then your effective amortization automatically becomes 25 years (providing the increase was made from your very first payment). You can't however select a 25 year amortization and then decide that you would be more comfortable with a lower payment amount and therefore reduce your payment to that of a 30 year amortization. It works one way, but not the other.

If you select a 30 year amortization but then set your payments as though it were 25 years, then your effective amortization automatically becomes 25 years

---

What I suggest for my clients really depends on their individual situation, goals, etc. If we are barely squeaking out an approval because the debt service ratios are so tight at 25 years, then it might be a good idea to consider 30 years if the option exists. This gives you added flexibility. You can try increasing your payments right after closing to see how you manage with the higher payment. If it feels like things are a little too tight, then you can always revert back to the original 30 year amortization, or anything in between.

Thanks to new mortgage regulations announced back in October of 2016, 30 year amortization is only available on uninsurable mortgages. For this reason, it often comes at a higher rate than what you can find with a 25 year. This can definitely make the choice a no brainer. If your mortgage is otherwise insurable, and you are dealing with a lender that doesn't offer you a lower rate for taking 25 years over 30 years, then chances are you may be missing out on lower rate options available elsewhere. For the differences between insurable and uninsurable mortgages, refer to the section entitled 'The New Age of Mortgages" found in Chapter One.

Anytime you make an extra payment on your mortgage, you are lowering your amortization and therefore paying less interest. I'll be talking more about strategies utilizing your prepayment privileges in Chapter Seven.

SHORT AMORTIZATION PERIODS

If you are in a situation where your mortgage payments are easily affordable, then you may want to consider going with a shorter amortization from the start. Many lenders have a minimum amortization of 10 years with some being as low as 5. With a shorter amortization, a much larger amount of your mortgage payment will go towards principal with a much smaller portion going towards interest. I'll be talking more about this in Chapter Seven.

CHAPTER TWO HIGHLIGHTS

- Consider your goals and your situation before choosing a mortgage term.
- 5 year terms are often more profitable for banks and brokers, so often this is what they push.
- 10 year fixed mortgages are even more profitable.
- 10 year fixed mortgages are an expensive gamble betting on the fact that rates will be skyrocketing. You would need to stay in for the entire 10 years to even have a slight chance of it working out in your favour.
- The choice between fixed and variable depends on your risk threshold.
- Just because variable has worked out for you in the past, it may not be the best option now.
- Always be mindful of the spread between fixed and variable before making your choice. A thinner spread means elevated risk.
- Consider a shorter term as an alternative to variable.
- If unsure whether to go with a 25 or 30 year amortization, consider the 30 and then set your payments based on the 25. It works out identical to a 25 year. You can always revert back to the lower payment if needed.
- If your debt-service ratios are particularly low, consider going with a shorter amortization.

Choosing the wrong product can cost you thousands of dollars unnecessarily. Either by paying a higher interest rate, or by paying a penalty to break the mortgage early if too long of a term was selected. Ask your mortgage professional for advice, but be mindful of whose best interest he or she has in mind. Think carefully about your situation before making a final decision.

Choosing a product is one part of the choice. Another is choosing the right lender, which is what we will be talking about next.

CHAPTER THREE

CHOOSING
THE RIGHT LENDER

THERE USED TO BE A time when you would head down to your local bank when you needed a mortgage. This is an old school mentality and things have certainly changed for the better. With the introduction of mortgage brokers back in the 1970's, the banks now have lots of competition with brokers capturing approximately 34% of overall mortgage business.[1]

---

1   Source: Mortgage Professionals Canada (Formerly the Canadian Association of Accredited Mortgage Professionals).

A LENDERS VS. B LENDERS

A lender can be classified as either an A lender or a B lender. An A lender is defined as one who deals with prime borrowers. Meaning borrowers with solid credit and provable, qualifying income. B lenders deal with the subprime borrowers. These are borrowers with less than perfect credit, un-provable income, or any borrower that does not fit within the parameters of an A lender's approval guidelines.

Some examples of A lenders are:

- First National
- Street Capital
- MCAP
- Industrial Alliance
- Any of the big banks

Some examples of B lenders are:

- Home Trust
- Equitable Bank
- Equity Financial Trust
- Effort Trust

Some B lenders such as Home Trust and Equitable Bank also have A divisions, however they are mostly known for their B side. MCAP on the other hand also has a B division, however they are mostly known for their A side.

In this chapter, I'll be focusing on A lenders and will be talking about B lenders in depth in Chapter Eight.

There are three types of A lenders in Canada. Big banks, local credit unions, and monoline lenders. As credit unions have many similarities to big banks, I'll be referring to them periodically in the bank lender section below.

BANK LENDERS

For many people, getting a mortgage with a big bank seems like the logical option. After all, banks have a recognizable brand name and there are locations on every urban street corner. If you're like many, you probably asked your parents for advice when considering buying your first home. The advice they likely gave was to head down to the bank and talk to them about it.

The big banks are often referred to as 'the big six':

- Scotiabank
- TD
- RBC
- National Bank
- CIBC
- BMO

The familiarity of the brand name is the biggest reason why some people prefer banks, and there are some advantages to dealing with them.

ADVANTAGES TO BANKS

- Brand name recognition
- Branches with convenient access
- View all your accounts on the same page
- Access to additional products
- No need to bulk-insure mortgages

Brand name recognition

We see their television commercials, billboards, ads on the sides of buses, newspapers, magazines, banners on the internet, etc. Bank advertising is ubiquitous. It's unlikely you can go through a single day without being exposed to their advertising. Because they spend millions of dollars each year on advertising, big bank branding is among the most recognizable in Canada.

Branches with convenient access

With branches across the country, a face-to-face meeting can be easily arranged at a location convenient to you. If you prefer to talk mortgages sitting across the desk from a live person, then a lender with a network of branches can be a solid benefit.

View all your accounts on the same page

If you're getting your mortgage at the same bank where you have your accounts, you can view your mortgage balance on the same page you view your chequing, savings, RRSP, etc.

Believe it or not, I've seen people pay thousands more for this convenience.

Access to additional products

As your bank doesn't only deal in mortgages, they are able to offer you other products such as credit cards, lines of credit, personal loans, RRSPs, TFSAs, investments, etc.

No need to bulk-insure mortgages

There is one area where major banks truly excel over monolines. They don't need to bulk insure their mortgages.

Right.

What the heck does that mean to you?

In Chapter One, I explained about the three different mortgage insurers, CMHC, Genworth and Canada Guaranty. These insurers are of course involved in all high ratio mortgages, meaning any mortgage with a down payment of less than 20%. However, monoline lenders will insure not just high ratio mortgages, but most mortgages regardless of down payment. You could be purchasing a home with 70% down payment and they will still insure the mortgage. It's just that in situations where the down payment is 20% or greater, they cover the fee giving you the impression that there is no insurance premium involved. It's all done on the back end and most likely, you'll never know about it. Providing your mortgage approval situation falls within the guidelines of the insurer's, it really makes no difference to you.

100% irrelevant.

Where it makes a difference is on deals that don't conform with the insurer's criteria. As major banks and credit unions don't have to insure their mortgages with 20% or more down payment, they have a lot more flexibility in what can be done.

This doesn't mean that they don't care about credit, income, or job history. It just means they can sometimes venture outside the insurer's imposed guidelines.

For example, let's say you have a home worth $500,000 and you own it free and clear. No mortgage and no money owing on it. You want to take out a mortgage of $300,000 to completely gut and renovate your home. As your home does not have a current mortgage that needs to be paid out, the entire $300,000 would be paid directly to you. This is referred to as an equity take out (as you are taking equity that is being paid directly to you). All three mortgage insurers have an equity take out limit of $200,000. Meaning, the maximum you would be able to borrow cannot exceed this amount. They are not paying out any mortgages or debt. Just $200,000 in cash going to you. Regardless of how much money you make or how much more you would qualify for. It doesn't matter, $200K is the limit. In this case, your only option will be to go with a major bank or credit union. Just to clarify, the $200,000 limit refers to the equity take out portion only. You can get a mortgage for higher amount, but the amount of cash being paid directly to you cannot exceed the $200,000 limit.

Another common example is debt service ratios. That is, your gross income in relation to the amount of debt you have. With monoline lenders, these debt service ratios are carved in stone. No flexibility at all. Where the total debt service ratio (TDS) limit is 44%, if you had 44.01%, then the approval would not be granted with a monoline lender (with the odd exception). With a bank, there 'may' be room to go higher on exception, providing you have a strong application.

Again, this applies only to mortgages with a down payment or equity position of 20% or greater. For the vast majority of borrower requirements, it's all the same either way, bank, credit union, or monoline.

DISADVANTAGES TO BANKS

- Higher rates
- Limited product availability
- Biased advice
- Higher penalties
- Limited branch hours

Higher rates

Some people prefer to deal with a major bank, and the banks know this. While sometimes you can get a great deal from a major bank, quite often their rates are higher than what can be obtained through a monoline lender or credit union. This is not always the case, but it's usually not a major bank that is leading the industry with the lowest rate.

Limited product availability / Biased advice

Wait a second… didn't I say an advantage to going with a big bank was that you had access to additional products? So how could this be an advantage….. and also a disadvantage?

In this case, I'm specifically talking about mortgage products alone.

When talking to a bank, you are limited to their products only. They don't have access to products from other lenders, so they are naturally going to be biased towards their own products and services. As these are the only products available to them, these are what they are going to sell you. They aren't going to come out and say, "hey, our rate is actually a little high on this, so you may want to check out X bank down the street who has as great special on right now."

Higher penalties

There also might be other pieces of important information they may not be so quick to disclose to you, such as certain terms or restrictions that make them different from other lenders. For example, collateral mortgages and higher penalties. You can't really blame them here. After all, if this is all they have to sell, then why are they going to sell against their own products?

All of the major banks have a harsher penalty calculation on fixed rate mortgages than what can be found with most monoline lenders. Also, some banks register all their mortgages as collateral charges. These banks may not be that quick to explain that their mortgages are registered differently than most other mortgage lenders, bank or non-bank.

I'll be discussing bank penalties and collateral mortgages in detail in Chapter Seven.

Limited branch hours

If you want to speak to the mortgage specialist at the bank, you're of course limited by that branch's hours. I remember a time when banks opened at 10am and closed at 4pm, Monday to Friday. Times have changed and now banks are open later, including weekends with some branches even having service on Sundays.

Many banks have now introduced mobile mortgage specialists so they can compete more with the service of a mortgage broker. However, when you walk into a branch to speak with someone about your mortgage, you're still going to be bound by branch hours.

MONOLINE LENDERS

Monoline lenders are institutions that only deal in one thing. Mortgages.

They are specialists in this field. Hence the name monoline. While that's the more strict definition, the term has come to be used for any mortgage lender that is not a bank or credit union. They aren't going to try to sell you a slew of other services after your mortgage closes. They don't offer RRSPs, investments, bank accounts, personal loans, or financing for anything other than real estate.

Here's a list of some of the more common monoline lenders in Canada:

- Street Capital
- First National
- Merix / Lendwise
- MCAP
- RMG Mortgages
- Canadiana Financial

Other lenders such as Industrial Alliance and B2B Bank offer other services as well as mortgages, so they are not mononline lenders, however they are still often categorized that way. Any lender who is not a chartered bank or credit union has come to be referred to as a monoline lender.

You may have never heard of these lenders, as they don't spend much on advertising. For the most part, they rely on the mortgage broker industry for promotion. This results in lower overhead allowing them to offer lower rates than the big banks in many cases.

While monoline lenders may be smaller than the big banks, they are heavily regulated and there is no additional risk when dealing with these lenders.

ADVANTAGES TO MONOLINE LENDERS

- Lower rates
- Lower penalties
- Specialists in mortgages only
- No post-closing sales pitches

Lower rates

In many cases, you can find lower rates with mononline lenders than with the big banks. The monoline lenders don't have branches to maintain, and their advertising budgets are minimal. This reduces their overhead cost which can then be passed on to the borrower.

Lower penalties

If you find yourself in a position where you need to break your mortgage early, penalties on variable rate mortgages are almost always 3 months interest. It doesn't matter if you are dealing with a bank or a monoline lender. The difference lies with fixed rates, which is where most monoline lenders have a much more consumer friendly penalty calculation. I'll be talking about this in detail in Chapter Seven.

Specialists in mortgages only

As already established, monoline lenders don't offer RRSPs, car loans, credit cards, investments, etc. They only deal in mortgages, which allow them to be experts in that field. When speaking to the lender directly, you can feel assured you are speaking with a mortgage expert.

No post closing sales pitches

If you've had a mortgage with a major bank before, you know that you'll receive solicitation calls periodically to sell things like insurance or investments. As monoline lenders only offer mortgages, there is nothing else that they can sell you once the mortgage closes.

DISADVANTAGES TO MONOLINE LENDERS

- No branches
- Lack of familiarity
- Mortgages are bulk-insured

No branches

Unlike the chartered banks, monoline lenders do not have local branches, so face to face contact is not possible with the lender directly.

Lack of familiarity

I hear it all the time. "Oh, the lender is 'such and such'? Never heard of them." You've never heard of them as they aren't spending millions on advertising as the banks do. They rely primarily on the mortgage broker network for promotion, as this is where close to 100% of their business comes from.

Mortgages are bulk-insured

Monoline lenders insure most of their mortgages through one of the three mortgage default insurance providers (CMHC, Genworth or Canada Guaranty). As explained in the section on big bank advantages, this can lead to less flexibility in circumstances where you have 20% or more down payment. I spoke about this in more detail a few pages back and will be talking about it more in Chapter Seven.

As discussed in Chapter One, new mortgage regulations were announced back in October of 2016 restricting what can be done with bulk insured mortgages. This has forced some monoline lenders to seek out additional funding sources that no longer require them to insure, which gives them greater flexibility. However, this is still a fairly new direction for monolines. At the time of writing, we are literally weeks into the new policies. Time will tell as to whether the monolines will allow for the same type of flexibility that can be found with big banks on uninsurable mortgages.[1]

MYTHS ABOUT MONOLINE LENDERS

There are many myths about monoline lenders :

- Extra or hidden fees.
- Miss a payment and the lender will take your house.
- If the lender goes out of business then you will be facing a big headache and have to pay all sorts of fees to get out of it.

Nothing of course could be further from the truth.

There are no extra or hidden fees when dealing with a monoline lender over a big bank. There are no additional costs whatsoever.

If you happen to miss a payment, you'll be subject to a late payment charge, which is no different when missing a payment to a bank. They aren't going to take your house. Regardless of the lender, they have no interest in this, nor are they legally eligible to do so even if they wanted to.

If the small lender happens to go out of business, their mortgage portfolio would just get taken over by another lender. All the same terms and conditions would remain in place. The only change you would notice is the logo on your mortgage statement. In August 2012, ING Bank sold their Canadian division to Scotiabank to raise

---

1   Refer to the section entitled "The New Age of Mortgages" in Chapter One for more information on the additional restrictions placed on bulk-insured (insurable) mortgages.

needed capital by their parent company. They were rebranded as Tangerine 18 months later and this was the only change their existing clients would have noticed.

If the small lender happens to go out of business, their mortgage portfolio would just get taken over by another lender. All the same terms and conditions would remain in place.

Also, some of these 'small' lenders are also quite large.

Industrial Alliance is a publicly traded company and has been around for over 130 years. As of 2016, they have over $100 billion in assets under their management.

RMG Mortgages is owned by the much larger MCAP, who is partially owned by BMO.

Even Merix Financial, who is one of the newer mortgage lenders (established in 2005) has over $20 billion in assets under their management.

The verdict?

Spending thousands of dollars more to go with a major bank doesn't make a lot of sense financially. There are ZERO added risks to going with a non-bank lender. The only real benefit to you is that you can have all your accounts with the same institution and can view them all on the screen together. Not much more.... other than recognizing the logo on your mortgage statement.

There are ZERO added risks to going with a non-bank lender.

There are some people that want to deal with a major bank no matter what the cost. This is usually due to myths or erroneous beliefs. Many people feel secure knowing their mortgage is held with a brand name institution. The truth is, their mortgage isn't any more secure with a major bank than it would be with any of the monoline lenders, big or small. I've seen people consciously spend over $10,000 more over a 5 year term just to have the privilege of giving the bank their business. Is it any wonder banks have the largest buildings in every city.

WHO'S HANDLING YOUR MORTGAGE FOR YOU?

What's more important than the institution you deal with is the person you hire to handle your mortgage for you. You have the choice of dealing directly with a big bank or dealing through a broker to access monoline lenders (as well as banks and credit unions).

There are good and bad on both the bank side and the broker side, so make sure you ask a lot of questions. You can have a great experience dealing with your mortgage or you can have a nightmare, which is why it is never a good idea to choose based on rate alone. I'll be talking more about this in the next chapter.

CHAPTER THREE HIGHLIGHTS

- An A lender is any lender who deals with qualified applicants with qualifying income and credit.
- A B lender deals with applicants who would not qualify through an A lender.
- Three main types of A lenders are banks, monoline lenders and credit unions.
- Common myths about non-bank lenders are that they have hidden fees and additional restrictions. That they will take your house if you miss a payment, or if they go out of business, you'll be left with a headache and additional costs. Nothing could be further from the truth.
- There is zero risk associated with getting your mortgage through a non-bank lender.
- Some of the smaller lenders are actually quite large and have billions of dollars in assets under their management.
- More importantly than your choice of lender is the person you choose to arrange your mortgage for you.

There is certainly nothing wrong with going with a bank and certainly nothing wrong with going with a non-bank lender. Banks definitely have their place and serve their purpose, as do non-bank lenders. One thing is for sure, if it were not for these non-bank lenders, the big banks would have a monopoly and free-reign to set the rates wherever they choose. Fortunately, there are options.

Now that we have a clear idea on the type of lending institutions out there, it's time to take a closer look at who is going to handle your mortgage for you.

CHAPTER FOUR

CHOOSING A MORTGAGE PROFESSIONAL

YOUR CHOICE OF MORTGAGE PROFESSIONAL can be just as important as your choice of lender. You can have a great experience dealing with your mortgage or you can have an absolute nightmare, solely based on the individual you select to handle everything for you. I've detailed the pros and cons of dealing with different types of institutions in the last chapter, so here I'll be focusing more on the individual you choose to arrange your mortgage.

There are two options. You can either deal with your bank directly or you can choose to go with a mortgage broker. According to a 2016 consumer survey conducted by Mortgage Professionals Canada, 51% of first time homebuyers obtained their mortgage through a broker.

WHAT IS A MORTGAGE BROKER?

The definition of a broker is one who brings the borrower and lender together. It's a common misconception that anyone dealing with mortgages is a mortgage broker. Nothing could be further from the truth. There is a big difference between a mortgage broker and a mortgage specialist working for a bank. A broker doesn't represent any one specific financial institution. Instead, he represents many. As the specialist at the bank works for a lender, he is not a broker as he isn't able to offer you mortgage products from any other institution other than their own. When shopping with a broker, you're shopping many different institutions at one time, and there lies the difference.

PROS TO DEALING WITH A BROKER

- More options
- Unbiased advice
- Convenience
- Free service
- Ease of access
- Licensed

More options

As brokers deal with multiple mortgage lenders, they have a lot more options open to them. This also gives you the ability to shop multiple lenders with just a single credit check, which can save you a lot of legwork. Brokers will often have options you'd never even think of, for all different types of financial situations.

Unbiased advice

When dealing with a bank, they can only talk about their products and their services. They are not going to tell you if there is another option available through a different lender that may be better suited to you. Brokers deal with non-bank lenders as well as some major banks, so they can tell you specifics about each lender and what makes one better than another. For the most part, it doesn't matter which lender the broker puts you with.

That being said, never just assume you're getting the right advice just because you're dealing with a broker. I've mentioned it before and I'll mention it again, there are good and bad on both sides. There are some products that may pay the broker a bit more than others, so some brokers may try to steer you to those products. This can happen on the bank side as well, as they may encourage their staff to push products that make them more money. Always analyze the reasoning for why the broker is suggesting a specific product over another and then make your own decision from there.

Convenience

Your mortgage can often be completely set up by phone and email without ever having to leave home. Perfect for anyone with a busy lifestyle. If you still prefer a face to face meeting, this can often be done in the broker's office or sometimes even within the comfort of your own home.

Free service

For qualified borrowers, using a mortgage broker doesn't cost anymore than it does to get a mortgage directly through your bank. In other words, it's free. Brokers get paid a finders fee from the lender, so it's a cost that you don't need to cover.

In cases where you don't qualify for financing through traditional sources, a broker may have to look at alternative financing in order to get you approved. If the broker can find a solution acceptable to you, then there may be additional fees involved, particularly if you are dealing with private mortgages. I'll be talking more about alternative financing and fees in Chapter Eight.

Ease of access

Mortgage brokers are not tied to any set schedule and have no set hours. It's commonplace for them to be working evenings, weekends and even holidays. It's not uncommon for me to be returning emails on Christmas Day.

Banks are now starting to introduce a mobile sales force as well, so in some cases you may also be able to get this same ease of access with a bank.

Licensed

Unlike mortgage specialists working for banks, mortgage brokers have licensing requirements that need to be met. In the province of Ontario for example, there are two types of licenses. Mortgage agent and mortgage broker. Both of which have to re-license every two years. The mortgage agent works directly for the mortgage broker. If someone wants to become a broker, they have to become a mortgage agent first. They must hold their agent license for a minimum of two years before they can become a broker, which requires twice as much training.

Does that mean you should only look at brokers because they have more training?

Definitely not!

There are some fantastic mortgage agents out there. I'll be talking more about how to select the right person later in this chapter.

These designations as mentioned apply to Ontario only and other provinces may have similar designations. BC for example has the mortgage broker and then the sub-broker (mortgage agent). While the designations are different, the concept is similar.

CONS TO DEALING WITH A BROKER

- No access to certain lenders
- Limited to no product availability outside mortgages
- No other point of contact
- Inconvenient location

No access to certain lenders.

Lenders such as BMO, CIBC and RBC do not deal directly with mortgage brokers, so in order to access these lenders you would need to access them directly.

Limited to no product availability outside mortgages

If you already have a mortgage and are looking to add a HELOC to it for example, a broker has very limited, if any options. In this case, you would need to deal with the lender directly. Other products that can't be obtained through brokers would be any type of personal or business loan, personal line of credit, etc.

No other point of contact

In many cases, if the broker doesn't get back to you right away or stops returning your calls for any reason, you may have difficulty getting someone else on the phone. Always make sure you know which brokerage he's working for and that you have the contact information for the brokerage as well. Many brokers work out of their homes and only give out their personal contact info. While each broker legally has to belong to a brokerage, it may be hard to find someone else who has access to your file.

Inconvenient location

Your broker may not be located as close to you as the bank, or they may not have a brick and mortar office at all. Many, if not most mortgage transactions can be done completely by phone, fax and email, so the need to meet in person is becoming less of an issue for many.

WHAT IS A BANK MORTGAGE SPECIALIST

A bank mortgage specialist is not a broker as they work specifically for one lender. A broker on the other hand, works independently from the lender and is not tied to any specific lender, as already discussed.

There is also a difference between dealing with your bank and dealing with a mortgage specialist at the bank. A mortgage specialist is exactly as the name implies. A specialist in mortgages. However, it's not uncommon for banks to have other staff selling mortgages as well. Someone recently told me they were dealing with the bank manager on their mortgage simply because she was their point of contact at that branch for years. A bank manager isn't necessarily a mortgage specialist. In fact, he may not be a mortgage expert at all.

The only way you can ensure you're dealing with a specialist is to ask questions to confirm they know their stuff. There are some really great specialists out there. Just make sure you're dealing with one so you can feel confident that everything will run smoothly and that you get the right answers to your questions. Never assume that just because you're dealing with someone at the bank that you're getting the right advice. I'll be talking more about the questions you should be asking later in this chapter.

PROS TO DEALING WITH A BANK MORTGAGE SPECIALIST

- Face to face contact
- Convenience
- Access to additional staff

Face to face contact.

While this can be done with your broker as well, it's more commonly done when dealing directly with your bank. This could also be looked at as a con as it requires you to set up a meeting to go over documents where as with a broker everything can be done by phone, fax or email.

Convenience

If you choose to meet face to face, you can find someone at a branch close to your residence or workplace.

Access to additional staff

If you have a complaint about the bank agent, there is always a manager you can speak with. If your contact suddenly goes on vacation while your mortgage is in progress, there are always others who can take over your file. A good mortgage broker would also ensure his files are covered when he goes on vacation. However, if someone were to leave for vacation without telling you, it may be easier to find someone else to review your file when dealing with a bank.

CONS TO DEALING WITH A BANK MORTGAGE SPECIALIST

- Limited availability
- Limited products
- Not licensed
- Limited alternatives

Limited availability

When you're dealing with a mortgage specialist at the branch, you're limited to dealing with them during their hours of operation. Not to mention, during the specialist's schedule within those hours. If you have any pressing questions or concerns about your mortgage, you'll have to wait until your contact returns to work.

As mentioned previously, some banks are now starting to introduce 100% commissioned mobile mortgage specialists to solve this problem. They are similar to brokers in the way that they are often available after hours and on weekends. The fact that they are 100% commissioned gives them more motivation to be available for you when you need them.

Limited products

As they work for the bank directly, they are only able to offer products from that one specific bank. If there is another product available from another institution, such as a lower rate or a product with better terms and conditions, they would not be able to offer it. Even if they know about it, they're certainly not going to tell you as it's not in their employer's (the banks) best interest. In other words, they are not going to send you to their competitor, which is perfectly understandable of course.

Not licensed

Unlike mortgage brokers, bank mortgage specialists do not have licensing requirements. There is no way to know what kind of training they have been provided with. If you are dealing with someone who is competent, then it's irrelevant, but it's another reason to make sure you ask a lot of questions before choosing to work with that person.

That being said, being licensed doesn't guarantee you're dealing with a competent individual by any means. You'll still need to ask a lot of questions before you can feel comfortable working with them, which I will be discussing shortly.

Limited alternatives

If you don't qualify for a mortgage due to credit, income or any other influencing factor, then they typically don't have any other options for you. As they work for just one lender, they have nowhere else to take you to.

The verdict?

Go to a bank and a broker and get a feel for both. See what they might be able to offer you individually. The most important thing is that you feel comfortable with the person you choose to handle your mortgage for you. Never choose to work with someone solely because you recognize the logo on their business card.

Paul Meredith

WHO ARE YOU GOING TO WORK WITH?

Now that you have a good feel for the pros and cons of each, you'll need to determine exactly whom you want to work with. I'm not talking about bank or broker. I'm talking about the actual individual you choose to deal with. You can have a great experience, or an experience from hell if you don't choose the right person... regardless of which side you choose to handle your mortgage for you.

Don't necessarily use the first person you speak with. Talk to multiple banks and brokers and then go with the one you feel most comfortable with. Incompetence is something that is common in this industry and can be experienced equally on both the bank and broker side.

Never assume you're in good hands just because you're dealing with your bank.

Never assume you're in good hands because you're dealing with a licensed broker.

You want to be dealing with a professional who is knowledgeable and going to take the time to listen to your needs and present your options to you based on your goals. As your mortgage is an important decision, make sure you are dealing with a professional who is competent and can get your mortgage closed with as little stress as possible.

Make sure you are dealing with a professional who is competent and can get your mortgage closed with as little stress as possible.

Several years ago, I had a client who left me to go to their bank, even though the bank had a higher rate. They said that the specialist at the bank was telling them that they didn't need to provide all the documents I was asking for. In fact, the documentation being requested was quite minimal. I tried to explain to them that the bank was going to need all the same documents and that they just hadn't asked for them yet. The clients didn't listen to me and went with their bank. Later they were scrambling to come up with the documents the day before closing, which was when the bank rep started asking for them. As a result, their home purchase ended up closing late, and the client incurred a lot of unnecessary stress.

My point is, competence is hugely important, so take the time to ensure your mortgage is in good hands.

So how do you determine you are in good hands? Simple… just ask a lot of questions.

One of the biggest mistakes someone can make is choosing a mortgage professional based on rate alone. It doesn't matter if you are going through a mortgage broker or through the mortgage specialist at a big bank. Make sure you ask a lot of questions to ensure you feel comfortable with the individual who is handling your mortgage.

One of the biggest mistakes someone can make is choosing a mortgage professional based on rate alone.

10 QUESTIONS TO ASK WHEN SELECTING A MORTGAGE PROFESSIONAL

1. How long have you been doing this for?

I would look for someone who has been in the business full-time for at least a couple of years. If they have been doing it less than that then it doesn't necessarily mean they are bad, but you may want to ask a few more questions. You can also ask how many mortgages they have closed and who they are working under. Make sure they have a go to person who is qualified if they don't have all the answers. If they don't know the answer to something, find out how long it might take for them to get the answers for you.

Like anyone else you're considering, you want to get a feel for them and their knowledge, and make sure you do your own research on their advice.

2. Do you do this full or part time?

I don't suggest dealing with anyone who is in the business part time, or anyone who has their time split between mortgages and anything other than mortgages. You want to ensure you are dealing with a specialist. The person you are working with should be fully committed to working on your mortgage. Their mind should be on you and not on their other income source. It is also very unlikely that a part-timer would have that much experience and you may have trouble reaching them if they are busy working their full-time job.

3. Do you have any references or testimonials?

It is always good to know that the professional you choose has a history of satisfied clients. If they have done a good job for their clients in the past, there is a better chance that they will do a great job for you as well.

4. What kind of education or licensing do you have?

Some professionals will have more education or training than others. As mentioned previously, brokers are licensed and bank specialists are typically not. Not being licensed isn't what I would call a deal breaker, but you definitely want to get a feel for what kind of training that person has been provided with. Chances are if they have been specializing in mortgages for years, then they should have a pretty good grasp on things. Just never make that assumption without feeling them out first.

5. How easy are you to get a hold of? How quickly do you return calls or emails?

There are going to be times when you have questions or concerns, and you are going to want to have them answered quickly. I've heard stories from my clients where they have been leaving messages for their mortgage broker or bank mortgage specialist for days or even weeks without a response. Not exactly what I would call professional or courteous service. I can't imagine how any 'professional' can even go three hours without responding to a question, yet alone days.

6. What hours are you available?

It can be helpful to know that the person you are dealing with can be flexible and is willing to work with YOUR schedule, not theirs. If you're typically not available or hard to reach during the day, then you might want to consider using someone who is available at times convenient to you. Having questions answered promptly will give you a significantly better experience. It's not fun when you have a concern and your mortgage professional is unreachable.

7. How do you get most of your business?

Ideally, most of their business should come from referrals and repeat business. You want to know that past clients are happy enough with their services that they are referring them to their friends and family. If a professional isn't doing a very good job for their clients, then they aren't going to have too many referrals.

8. How are fixed mortgage rates determined?

This is simply a question to gauge their competence level and is something that any quality mortgage professional will know right away. If they can't answer this, or if they have to 'get back to you', then I would move on to the next person. (The answer is bond yields.)

9. Do you do anything else for the branch other than mortgages?

This question is for bank branch staff only and does not apply to mortgage brokers. The goal here is to determine you are dealing with a true mortgage specialist. If they also tell you they do financial planning, then they are not a true specialist. Make sure you are dealing with someone where they specialize in mortgages and mortgages only.

10. How many different lenders do you deal with?

This question is for brokers only. Many brokers will advertise that they have access to over 30 different lenders. While the brokerage they work for may have access to this many lenders in some cases, it's pretty much impossible for any single broker to actually use this many. Anything over 10 would be tough to maintain as it can be a challenge to keep track of that many lenders and their products. Six or seven is a more realistic number. In the province of Ontario, the number of lenders the brokerage has dealt with in the past year needs to be disclosed in the approval documents. While someone telling you they have access to over 30 lenders shouldn't necessarily eliminate them as an option, a better question to ask would be this:

How many lenders have you dealt with in the past year?

There are some brokers out there who will filter all their business through only one lender. I call these people 'non-brokers'. While they hold a brokers license, and work on the broker side, they aren't doing the job of a broker considering they are only dealing with one lender. Having access to multiple lenders is one of the big benefits to dealing with a broker, so this would eliminate that benefit.

So why would a broker choose to deal with only one lender?

Some lenders may give out points, or extra commission to that broker once they have reached a certain level with them. Filtering all their clients through a single lender is a sign that they may not be offering their clients the best options and that they may not have your best interests in mind. A broker may say he has access to 30 different lenders, however that doesn't mean he's submitting deals to all of them. You can press a little further and ask which lender he deals with the most and what percentage of his business goes to that lender. In Ontario, the broker has to disclose if his brokerage has placed over 50% of his business with one lender. If this is the case, I would question why they are sending so much business to a single lender.

CHAPTER FOUR HIGHLIGHTS

- Who you choose to handle your mortgage for you can be more important than your choice of lender.
- When choosing someone to handle your mortgage for you, there are two options. Dealing with the bank directly or dealing with a mortgage broker.
- A broker is one who brings the borrower and lender together and does not work for any one specific lender. Therefore, the mortgage specialist at your bank is not a mortgage broker.
- Talk to multiple banks and brokers and then go with the one you feel most comfortable with.
- Incompetence is something that is common in this industry and can be experienced equally on both the bank and broker side.

- Ask a lot of questions to ensure you're dealing with a knowledgeable and confident professional.
- One of the biggest mistakes you can make is choosing someone to work with based on rate alone.

The importance of choosing the right person to handle your mortgage for you cannot be stressed enough. The biggest nightmare of an incompetent mortgage professional is a knowledgeable client. Arming yourself with knowledge prior to your meeting with the mortgage professional will make it all that much easier to choose.

Your meeting could be in person or it could be on the phone. Either way, you'll want to get yourself prepared for it, which is what we will be discussing next.

CHAPTER FIVE

PREPARE FOR YOUR MEETING

W HEN MEETING WITH A BROKER or a bank for the first time, whether it be on the phone or in person, it can help to go in armed with knowledge. This will help you to better understand what's being discussed at the meeting and will allow you to speak more freely about it. An informed shopper will keep the mortgage professionals on their toes.

HOW ARE MORTGAGES QUALIFIED?

The first thing the mortgage professional will want to determine is how much you'll qualify for. There are some people that automatically assume they will qualify for a mortgage. Never make this assumption and always visit a mortgage professional first to get pre-approved.

There are four components that are considered when determining how much you'll qualify for.

- Down payment
- Credit
- Income
- Debt

Each of these components can be complex in their own way, so let's take a closer look at them in detail to give you a solid understanding of each one.

DOWN PAYMENT

As discussed back in Chapter One, having a down payment of 20% or more will save you from having to pay mortgage default insurance (CMHC). It will also allow you to extend your amortization to 30 years. A longer amortization will allow you to qualify for a higher mortgage amount considering it lowers your mortgage payments. This applies to uninsurable mortgages only.[1]

---

1   Refer to the section entitled "The New Age of Mortgages" in Chapter One for more information on the difference between insurable and uninsurable mortgages.

The source of your down payment is taken very seriously by all institutional mortgage lenders, bank, credit union, or monoline. This is because it must be in compliance with the Proceeds of Crime (Money Laundering) and Terrorist Financing Act, which is why you'll find they are all quite stringent when it comes to documentation to support your down payment.

Acceptable forms of down payment include:

- Chequing / savings accounts
- RRSP
- Gifts from immediate family (parents or sibling)
- Secured line of credit

Unacceptable forms of down payment include:

- Cash 'under the mattress'
- Gifts from friends or extended family
- Loans from friends or family (immediate or not)
- Bank loans
- Unsecured line of credit
- Credit cards
- Any money that can't be traced or explained (Typically any amount over $1,000)

The documentation required to support the down payment is bank and/or investment statements for the past 90 days to show the natural accumulation of the funds. Any large deposits need to have documentation to support them. It's not uncommon for some people to transfer money from one account to another. In these cases, even if all your funds are in one account and ready to go, ninety days of statements will also be required on the other accounts to show the origin of the transferred funds. In the event that the deposit does not have an acceptable explanation or cannot be supported by an acceptable source, then those funds cannot be used towards the down payment.

If the entire down payment and closing costs are from the sale of a recently sold property within the past 90 days, then bank statements for the entire period are typically not required. The lender would request the trust ledger you received from your lawyer showing how much funds were disbursed to you on closing. You would also need to provide a bank statement showing those funds being deposited into your account.

CREDIT

The second key component in determining qualification is your credit. Never assume your credit is solid. It's not uncommon for a credit bureau to contain 'surprises'. Sometimes there may be collections from past debts you swore were paid that could come back to haunt you. Or mistakes made by creditors that need to be corrected. It's also possible that Equifax (the credit reporting agency used by most brokers and lenders) could have multiple files on you… meaning, multiple credit bureaus. Your mortgage professional should take the time to go over your credit bureau with you to ensure everything is accurate and that there is nothing missing. Should you be in a situation where there are multiple files under your name, your mortgage professional will be able to get this corrected for you quite easily.

Your credit score is referred to as your 'beacon score' when pulled by a mortgage professional through Equifax. If you pull your credit bureau yourself, then it is referred to as your 'FICO' score. These scores are calculated differently and you could have a beacon score that's quite different from your FICO score. In the end, **the beacon score is the only one that matters.**

The beacon score gives lenders a quick indication of your credit worthiness and can be the make or break factor on many mortgage approvals. The score ranges from 300-900 with 300 being the worst and 900 being the best. Any score under 620 is considered to be 'poor credit' while anything under 550 drops the status from poor to bad. Credit scores between 620 and 660 are considered fair, while credit scores between 660 and 679 are considered good. Anything over 680 is excellent. Whether you have a score of 680 or a score of 800 is irrelevant for qualification purposes in most situations and having a particularly high score doesn't get you any special privileges.

I'll be talking more about credit score later in this chapter.

Thin Credit

Just because you have a solid credit score does not mean you have solid credit. You can have a credit score of 850 and still be declined based on credit.

WHAT? That doesn't make sense!

I'd have to agree, but some things in this industry don't always make the most sense at first glance. The reasoning behind it is that without enough history to support the credit score there is insufficient evidence to accurately demonstrate credit responsibility. In other words, mortgage lenders want to see that you have enough credit to show you're able to handle it and have had it for long enough to adequately prove this to them.

The general requirement is to have two active trade lines, each showing a minimum history of at least one year. Some lenders require two years. A trade line is a credit card, line of credit or loan that reports on your credit bureau. It's preferred that both (or at least one) of the trade lines be revolving. That is, a trade line where you can re-access the credit limit after it's paid down, such as a credit card or line of credit.

> *The general requirement is to have two active trade lines, each showing a minimum history of at least one year.*

The limit on each revolving trade line should be at least $1,000, however higher limits are preferred. There is a common belief that too much credit is considered bad, and for this reason, some will try to keep their credit as thin as possible. While having excessive credit could be a concern for mortgage lenders, it would have to be quite excessive for you to be turned down based on available credit alone. However, getting declined due to thin credit is much more common. The reasoning here is that thin credit doesn't accurately portray a solid demonstration of credit responsibility.

For example, lets say you closed all your credit cards and had no active loans on your credit bureau. You may have a high credit score reporting, but since there is nothing active, then you would certainly be declined. If the same credit report had a $300 credit card that was just added three months ago, then you would still be declined for a mortgage. This is because there is only three months of 'active' history. The key word here is 'active'.

Mortgages didn't start reporting on credit bureaus until 2015 for some strange reason. You would think a loan as large as this would be the first thing reporting! Even though it's now listed, it doesn't count as a trade line, nor does it even count towards your score. Weird, I know.

INCOME

Mortgage lenders of course need to see a sustained capacity to support the payments on the loan. In other words, a steady flow of income high enough to support the overall debt, as well as a sufficient history of earnings. The documentation required to support income can vary depending on the income source.

Salaried Workers

For salaried workers, the requirements are usually just a recent pay stub and recent job letter showing your position, start date and annual income. If there's a non-guaranteed bonus structure to the income then this would need to be supported by your last two years Notice of Assessments (NOA).[1] It is the average of your line 150 over the past two years that would be used as your income.

Hourly Workers

Providing that you are guaranteed a specific amount of hours, a job letter and pay stub may be all that is required. Providing of course your hours can be confirmed as guaranteed. This would be verified by your job letter and pay stub, as well as with a verbal

---

1   The NOA is what the Canada Revenue Agency sends out each year about six weeks after you do your taxes.

confirmation the lender will get from your employer closer to closing. In some cases, depending on the lender, your last two years NOAs may still be required, even with guaranteed hours. If your hours are not guaranteed, then your last two years NOAs will almost certainly be required.

Commissioned Sales

If there is a commission component to your earnings then your last two years NOAs are required to support your income. Just as with using bonus income above, it's the average of your line 150 for the past two years that will be used. A job letter and a pay stub will still be required as well. In some rare cases, a T4 may be requested, however a T4 can generally not be used as a substitute for an NOA and is not something that is typically accepted.

A full two year history with the same employer is required if any overtime, commission, or bonus income is to be considered. If you are under two years with your employer, then only your base income or guaranteed hours can be used.

Self-Employed

The process is a little different for self-employed borrowers, after all, you're not going to write your own job letter. Well, you can try if that's what makes you happy, but it's not going to get you anywhere. Providing you can prove you have been in business for at least two years, then your self-employed income can be considered at the lowest market mortgage rates.

There are two different categories that income from self-employed individuals can be put into. Documented and undocumented. Documented income would be income that can be supported by your last two years NOAs. In many cases, the average of your line 150 for the past two years can be grossed up by 15%. The reason for this is that it is understood that as a self-employed individual, you'll likely have additional write offs resulting in lower, provable income compared with what's actually earned.

Where you will not qualify based on documented income, you may still be able to get approved under the undocumented income category. This is where a much larger portion of your actual income is hidden, leaving you with too low of an income to qualify. This can be either due to tax write offs or due to having a larger cash component to the business, which is commonly found with trade workers. Undocumented income can be a little more complicated, however it can often still be done. In these cases, you would state a reasonable amount of income for your profession, which would require limited documentation to support it. In some cases, with no documentation at all. This is more commonly referred to as a stated income mortgage.

Before the US real estate crash in 2008, it was possible to do stated income mortgages with no evidence at all to support it. It was seldom even questioned, providing it was reasonable. Obviously if a self-employed hair stylist is stating $250,000 in income while only reporting $20,000 on his NOA, then this would of course be unreasonable. However if the same hair stylist were stating $40,000 in income with $20,000 showing on his NOA, then it would be much easier to make a case for him. After all, he would get paid a certain amount in cash tips, not to mention all his write offs for items required in the day-to-day operation of his business.

While all mortgage lenders will accept a qualified, self-employed applicant with documented income, not every lender has a stated income program, so options are more limited. In some cases, it can still be just as easy to qualify for a stated income mortgage, providing everything makes sense. Proof of self-employment is always required, as a lender will definitely want to confirm that this is in fact what you do for a living. A business license or articles of incorporation are usually asked for. However, it's understood that these documents aren't always available, as not all legitimate businesses have to be registered. You can legally operate a business under your own name for example. In these cases, the following documents can be considered:

- Notice of Return Adjustment/Summary from the CRA (GST return)
- T1 Generals (tax return) for the past two years complete with a statement of business activities.
- Financial statements for the past two years prepared and signed by an accountant.

NOAs are always required on stated income mortgages... not to confirm income, but to confirm that there are no taxes owing.

Part-Time Income

There is a two-year minimum employment period required to consider part-time income with most lenders. The average of the last two years NOAs, job letter and pay stub are required for confirmation. In some cases, T4s are also requested.

DEBT

The last major factor considered in mortgage approval is your debt load. A small amount of debt won't have any effect on how much you qualify for, providing you are within the allowable debt service ratios. A debt service ratio is the amount of debt you carry in relation to your income level.

There are two debt service ratios involved with qualification. The Gross Debt Service Ratio (GDSR) and the Total Debt Service Ratio (GDSR). These are more commonly referred to as the GDS and TDS.

GDS

The GDS is your total mortgage payment including principal and interest, in addition to your property tax and heating costs (commonly written as PITH) divided by your income.

The formula looks like this:

$$\frac{\text{PITH (principal, interest, heat, taxes)}}{\text{Income}}$$

TDS

The TDS is your total mortgage payment, taxes and heat (PITH), plus the monthly payment on all your other debt, divided by your income. For traditional bank loans, either personal or for the purchase of a vehicle, the actual monthly payment is used for the debt service calculation. For credit card or line of credit balances, 3% of the balance is used, regardless of the actual amount owing, even if there are no payments required for a specified period.

The formula for the TDS looks like this:

$$\frac{\text{PITH} + \text{debt payments}}{\text{Income}}$$

Both the GDS and TDS can be calculated on a monthly basis or on an annual basis. Either way, the results are the same.

While heating is often an unknown and unprovable variable, most lenders will use $125 when calculating debt service ratios. For properties with a larger square footage, a higher amount may be used, depending on the lender.

In cases where there is a condo or maintenance fee, the fee gets calculated into the debt service ratio at 50% of the actual amount. In other words, if the condo fee were $400, only $200 would be used in these calculations. If the maintenance fee includes heat, as it sometimes does, then heating costs can be omitted.

The maximum GDS is 39% and the maximum TDS is 44%.

Let's break this down and see how it looks using real numbers. Let's say John and Mary Smith require a mortgage of $400,000 at 2.99% amortized over 30 years. (I'll leave off the pennies for simplicity).

Monthly payment (P&I): $1,680
Property tax (monthly): $250
Heat: $125
Total property related expenses: $2,055
Monthly household income: $5,500

Using these numbers, the formula for the GDS looks like this:

$$\frac{\$2,055 \text{ (PITH)}}{\$5,500}$$
$$\text{GDS} = 37.36\%$$

Assuming acceptable credit, they will qualify based on GDS as the ratio is below the maximum of 39%.

Now, let's toss in some debt, just for the fun of it. We'll tack on the following:

Car loan: $225 / month
Credit cards: $39 / month (3% of a $1,300 balance)
Line of credit: $60 / month (3% of a $2,000 balance)
Total monthly debt = $324

The formula for the TDS looks like this:

$$\frac{(\$2,055 + \$324)}{\$5,500}$$

$$TDS = 43.25\%$$

Our beloved borrowers John and Mary will qualify as their ratio is still under 44%...although it's tight.

HOW YOUR CREDIT SCORE IS DETERMINED

35% - Payment History

The biggest portion of your credit score is your ability to make your payments on time. How much you choose to pay towards your credit cards is irrelevant as long as you at least make the minimum payment. Some people may think, "I'll skip the payment this month but I'll make a much larger payment next month to make up for it".

NO!

The ONLY thing that matters is that you make your payment on time! Paying a bill even one day late can result in a late payment being reported. Make sure you pay your bills on time. An automatic bill pay system or a pre-authorized payment program can help with this tremendously.

30% - How Much You Owe

If you have all your credit cards maxed out, then this is going to negatively affect your score. Try to keep credit card balances under 75% of the limit if possible. The lower the better. Also try to control how much debt you carry. You can have a great score and qualifying income, however if your debt load seems excessive to a lender then you can still end up getting declined... even if everything else qualifies.

15% - Length of Credit History

This is the time since each account was opened and the time since its last activity. It is important to use cards periodically, rather than just let them sit. If you don't go to the gym periodically, your muscles will become soft and flabby. The same applies to your credit. Even putting $10 on a credit card once or twice a year will help keep your credit strong and healthy. If only the same could be said for going to the gym!

Cards that have been sitting dormant for years will not have any positive impact on your credit whatsoever. Your score may not suffer, but the strength of your credit bureau will. For example, let's say you have a total of three credit cards reporting and you haven't used them for a few years. You still may end up getting declined for a mortgage due to lack of recent credit history, regardless of how high your score may be.

10% - New Credit

This refers primarily to the number of accounts recently opened and the number of recent inquiries. Don't open up new credit accounts unless you need to. While credit checks will affect credit score, they are only one component in this category.

Many believe that their credit score will start plummeting the moment a potential creditor pulls your report. While it does drop, there is usually no need to worry about having someone check your credit, unless your credit is sitting right on the border. For example, if your score is 625 and then it drops to 615 after a couple of checks, then this could possibly mean the difference between qualification and decline. However if your score is 775 and a couple of checks drop it to 765, then it's 100% irrelevant. Your score would have to drop below 680 for it to make any difference. I'll be talking about why 680 is the magic number in the next section on debt service ratios.

On the other end of the stick, if your score is 450, which is pretty bad, then there is no point in worrying about someone checking your score. The damage is done. It doesn't matter if your score is 470 or 420, you still don't qualify for a traditional mortgage.

In the above examples, I'm using a ten point drop for demonstration purposes only. The actual amount your score drops from each check can vary depending on your circumstances, however in my experience, it's typically minimal in most situations where credit is healthy.

10% - Mix of Trade Lines

It is good practice to have a variety of trade lines. For example, instead of having all credit cards, have a line of credit, a credit card, a car loan... etc. Mixing it up a bit shows diversification, which can demonstrate better credit responsibility.

HOW RATE AFFECTS QUALIFICATION

There are two different rates that are used when determining the maximum mortgage amount you will qualify for. The contract rate and the benchmark rate. The contract rate is the rate your mortgage payment is based on (principal and interest exclusive of property taxes). The benchmark rate is set by the Bank of Canada, which is based on the posted rates from the big banks.

With variable rate mortgages, fixed rates with terms shorter than 5 years, and high ratio mortgages (less than 20% down payment), the benchmark rate is always used.

With variable rate mortgages, fixed rates with terms shorter than 5 years, and high ratio mortgages (less than 20% down payment), the benchmark rate is always used. This is the case regardless of mortgage lender. The benchmark rate is typically higher than the contract rate. So even though your actual rate and payment is lower, for qualification purposes, the higher rate is used which results in a lower qualified amount. For this reason, a 5 year fixed may be the only option available for borrowers if they are facing non-qualifying debt service ratios, providing they have at least 20% down payment. If their down payment is below 20%, then they'll have no choice but to qualify based on the higher rate, regardless of how much lower their actual payments may be.

The reasoning behind this is to protect you the borrower against rising future interest rates. At the time of writing, mortgage rates are near record lows. It's not a typical market where we have 5 year fixed rates beginning with a two. If a couple chooses a 2 year fixed for example, and their debt service ratios are maxed out based on contract rate, then it's unlikely their financial position will have changed much in two years time. This means, if rates are any higher at the end of two years, they may face serious financial difficulty as they struggle to make higher payments as a result of the higher rate. For that reason, regulation involving the higher qualifying rate was introduced to protect these borrowers in the future.

Some lenders will use the benchmark rate to qualify all their mortgages, regardless of how much you have available for down payment. This is due to new mortgage regulations that were announced back in October of 2016. Fortunately, there are still many that will qualify you based on the contract rate as long as you have a minimum down payment of 20%.

CHAPTER FIVE HIGHLIGHTS

- Arm yourself with knowledge. An informed shopper will help keep the mortgage professional on his toes.
- There are four basic components to mortgage qualification. Down payment, credit, income and debt.
- Never assume you will qualify for a mortgage.
- Having too much credit is better than not having enough credit.
- There are two ratios used in calculating debt service. The Gross Debt Service Ratio (GDS) and the Total Debt Service Ratio (TDS).
- Providing you have at least 20% down payment, 5 year fixed rates qualify based on the contract rate (the rate your payments are based on) where variable and shorter term mortgages have to qualify based on a much higher rate known as the benchmark rate. Those with a down payment under 20% will also have to qualify based on the benchmark rate.

The more knowledgeable you are going into your first meeting or telephone call, the better chance you'll have at gauging the experience level of the person handling your mortgage for you. A strong knowledge of how the approval process works combined with the information outlined in the last chapter will make your mortgage shopping much easier. This knowledge will also help you to choose a competent mortgage professional. It really is amazing just how little many so-called 'professionals' in this industry actually know. On both the bank and the broker side. If you know more than they do... then why would you choose them to handle your mortgage for you? Arm yourself with knowledge... and then shop with confidence.

CHAPTER SIX

DOWN PAYMENT STRATEGY

T HE FIRST THING TO CONSIDER when purchasing a home is how much you have available for down payment. This is also one of the first things the mortgage professional will ask you.

Do you put down the bare minimum? Or do you save up for more?

MINIMUM DOWN PAYMENT

The minimum down payment to purchase a home is 5% of the purchase price. This minimum down payment however is not as cut and dry as it used to be with the introduction of new regulation that took effect on February 15th, 2016.

The 5% minimum down payment applies only to purchases up to $500,000. For anything over $500,000, it is 10%, but only on the amount exceeding $500,000.

For example, if you are purchasing a home for $800,000, you'll need 5% for the first $500,000 and 10% on the remaining $300,000 making the minimum down payment on this purchase $55,000.

Breaking it down in terms of numbers, 5% of the first $500,000 is $25,000 and 10% of the remaining $300,000 is $30,000 for a total minimum down payment of $55,000.

For any purchase over $1,000,000, the minimum down payment is 20%.

As discussed in Chapter One, a purchase with a down payment less than 20% is considered a high ratio mortgage, therefore will require mortgage default insurance such as CMHC (see Chapter One for complete details on mortgage default insurance).

SHOULD MORTGAGE DEFAULT INSURANCE BE AVOIDED?

There is no question mortgage default insurance can be quite costly, but should it be avoided? As explained in Chapter One, its sole purpose is to protect the lender in the event the borrower defaults on the mortgage payments. The only benefit to the borrower is that it allows them to purchase a home with less than 20% down. In a hot market, this benefit can be huge.

I hear people who are not mortgage professionals trying to give advice all the time. Everyone thinks they're an expert and everyone is entitled to their own opinion of course. "Go with the lowest amortization possible, save up at least 20% before buying a home to save on the insurance premium!" While these options may be what's most suitable for them, they aren't universal by any means.

You'll want to observe how fast homes are appreciating in your area and compare that with how long you think it will take to save up the 20% down payment. Let's use the Greater Toronto Area as an example. From 2000 to 2014, the average home price in the GTA has appreciated an average of 6.26%, or $23,106 per year.

Let's say it's 2011 and Jim and Sandy Homebuyer are looking to purchase their first home in the GTA. They have 5% available for down payment, but they've heard that it's a good idea to save up 20% in order to avoid paying CMHC insurance. For this reason, they decide to wait until they have 20%, which takes them another three years to accumulate.

If they had purchased their home with 5% down in 2011 as they were originally considering, the average home price in the GTA was $465,014, which would have required a down payment of $23,250[1] (5%). The mortgage default insurance at the time was 2.75% (now 4.00%), which would have cost them $12,148 in insurance fees. As this gets added to the mortgage, the starting mortgage balance would have been $453,911.

The calculation looks like this:

Purchase Price − Down Payment + Insurance Premium = Mortgage Amount
$465,014 − $23,250 + $12,148 = $453,911

Let's say the interest was 2.99% and they amortized over 25 years. Their monthly payment would have been $2,146 and their balance after 3 years would have been $415,487 (assuming monthly payments).

Fast forward to 2014. Jim and Sandy now have their 20% down payment and are ready to shop for their first home.

The average home price in the GTA is now $566,696[2]... over $100,000 higher than it would have been if they had purchased in

---

1   I'm leaving the pennies off throughout this example for simplicity, so actual numbers may fluctuate by a dollar in either direction.

2   Source: Toronto Real Estate Board

2011. Their 20% down payment would be $113,339, which is $90,088 more than the 5% they would have put down in 2011. This means they would have had to save the equivalent of $2,500 per month over the past 3 years in order to avoid the insurance premium. Their starting balance would be $453,357.

This is $37,870 more than they would have owed if they had purchased in 2011 with only 5% down. Add on the money they would have saved for the 20% down payment and you have a difference of just under $128,000. If they were paying rent for the three years they spent saving for the 20% down payment, then this would add to the overall cost of waiting to purchase their home.

All this just so they could save $12,148 in CMHC fees.

As you can see, delaying a home purchase can be quite costly in a rising housing market.

Saving up the 20% down payment to avoid the CMHC premium can still be viewed as financially prudent. The above scenario was based on the Toronto market in a period that saw higher than normal appreciation. There are many smaller markets that will see significantly less. There are also periods where home prices can dip, depending on economic circumstances. You have to do what you feel most comfortable with and what you think makes sense for you.

Delaying a home purchase can be quite costly in a rising housing market.

BUT WHAT IF THE MARKET CRASHES?

Saving the mortgage default cost isn't the only reason why many suggest saving up the full 20% down payment. The other reason is to protect yourself against a market correction by having a larger equity position in your home. This way, if the market were to take a dive, you're still likely in the black… meaning, your home is still worth more than what you owe on it.

Sure, it's possible that the market could correct. Anything can happen. If you purchase with only 5% down, and if the market were to correct right after purchasing, you would end up owing more on your home than it's worth. That is… until the market starts appreciating again, as it would.

There is no shortage of doom and gloomers out there that are always predicting a housing market catastrophe. "It's a bubble waiting to pop!" I've been hearing these predictions since 2006 and they haven't stopped straight through to the time of writing in 2017. Anyone who listened to these people and either sold their homes, or waited for the big crash before purchasing would have missed out on potential six figure appreciation.

Will the market crash?

Anything can happen and no one can say for sure. Maybe it will or maybe it won't. All anyone can do is speculate. Time will tell.

One thing we know for sure is that homes in the GTA (as an example) have appreciated every single year from 1997 straight through to early 2017… and counting.

Year	Average Sale Price	Change ($)	Change (%)	Total Sales
1997	$211,307	+ $13,157*	+ 6.64%*	58,014
1998	$216,815	+ $5,508	+ 2.61%	55,344
1999	$228,372	+ $11,557	+ 5.33%	58,957
2000	$243,255	+ $14,883	+ 6.52%	58,343
2001	$251,508	+ $8,253	+ 3.39%	67,612
2002	$275,231	+ $23,723	+ 9.43%	75,759
2003	$293,067	+ $17,836	+ 6.48%	78,898
2004	$315,231	+ $22,164	+ 7.56%	83,501
2005	$335,907	+ $20,676	+ 6.56%	84,145
2006	$351,941	+ $16,034	+ 4.77%	83,084
2007	$376,236	+ $24,295	+ 6.90%	93,193
2008	$379,347	+ $3,111	+ 0.82%	74,552
2009	$395,460	+ $16,113	+ 4.25%	87,308
2010	$431,276	+ $35,816	+ 9.06%	85,545
2011	$465,014	+ $33,738	+ 7.82%	89,096
2012	$497,130	+ $32,116	+ 6.91%	85,496
2013	$522,958	+ $25,828	+ 5.20%	87,049
2014	$566,696	+ $43,738	+ 8.36%	92,829
2015	$622,116	+ $55,420	+ 9.78%	101,230

Source: Toronto Real Estate Board

*Average sale price in 1996 was $198,150

Average % increase each year: 6.24%

Average $ increase each year: $22,314

When you add on 2016 where numbers were up once again, that's twenty years with appreciation every single year (2016 numbers were not yet available at time of publication). So does this mean this trend can be expected to continue for the next twenty years? I would say that is an unrealistic prediction, as the real estate market will eventually correct. Whether this comes in the form of the market flattening out for a few years or whether it drops 5-10% or more remains to be seen. Maybe it will happen within the next couple of years, or maybe it won't happen for another 10 years. All anyone can do here is speculate. It's not guaranteed that real estate will increase every single year. Crashes are always a possibility.

So what do you do?

When coming to a decision on whether to purchase with a minimal down payment or whether you should wait to come up with 20% really depends on what you feel most comfortable with. You do need to ask yourself this one important question:

What is the reason you are purchasing your home?

Are you purchasing it to use as your primary residence for you and your family? If you are just looking for a roof over your head, and the market were to take a dip, how is this going to affect you?

If you ended up with a negative equity position in your home (owing more than it's worth) following a correction, the only negative impact on you (other than the obvious loss of equity) is that you may have to wait longer before selling your home. The market will eventually rebound and your equity will eventually come back. During the rebound, you will also continue to pay down your mortgage balance with each scheduled payment. If the thought of owing more on your home than what its worth scares you, then you may want to consider increasing your payments to build equity faster. I'll be talking more about this in the next chapter.

OTHER BENEFITS TO A SMALLER DOWN PAYMENT

If you do have the resources for a 20% down payment, does that mean you should definitely put down the full amount? As a mortgage broker, I see some people who are able to put more down, and in some cases, much more, yet they still choose to put down the minimum.

Why would anyone want to do this?

It comes down to what your other options are for the additional funds. At the time of writing, mortgage rates are at near record lows with both fixed and variable rate mortgages available well below 3%. You need to ask yourself if you think you can earn a higher return than your mortgage rate by investing the money instead.

How much do you think you'll be able to earn from your investments?

I am not a financial advisor, nor do I pretend to be, so you're not going to see me venturing outside of my area of expertise with personal advice on how to invest your money. However, before making a final decision on down payment, I do suggest speaking with a qualified financial advisor on what your other options might be. It's possible that you could end up with far more money at the end of your mortgage term than you would have if you had used the extra funds towards your down payment.

Before making a final decision on down payment, I do suggest speaking with a qualified financial advisor on what your other options might be

---

PURCHASING A HOME WITH NO MONEY DOWN

There used to be a time when just about anyone with a decent credit score could purchase a home with no money down. While options to purchase with no down payment are now much more limited, it's still possible. You're still going to need 5% down, however you can borrow this 5% if you have a line of credit with a large enough limit. So you would be financing 95% of the purchase with the mortgage secured against the home, with the remaining 5% borrowed against an unsecured line of credit.

Bingo!

You've just financed 100% of the purchase.

The payments for the borrowed down payment will need to be factored into the debt service ratios for qualifying. If you don't quite have 5% saved up and you are eager to purchase a home, then this can be an alternative providing everything makes sense for you.

Is this a good idea?

Many will advise against it, and I'm personally not a big fan of this strategy either. For that reason, I struggled with whether or not I should even include it in this book. As it is an option, and it's something that may work for certain individuals, I decided to include it.

So why isn't it recommended?

It's about having debt and being able to control it. Let's say you are purchasing a condo for $300,000 and are maxing out your line of credit with a $15,000 cash advance. Right off the bat, you have $15,000 in additional debt that you're now going to have to focus on paying off. Not the best way of starting out if you're struggling to make ends meet as it is.

Let's consider the following situation where this strategy may be an option to consider.

Joe and Flo Schmo are looking at purchasing their first home, yet don't have any funds accumulated for down payment. They have about $10,000 saved up which they can use towards their closing costs, but they won't have anywhere close to the $20,000 they will need to purchase the $400,000 home they are interested in buying. The market is hot with values appreciating an average of 8% per year. Waiting an extra year would mean they would have to spend an additional $32,000 to purchase a similar home.

Joe is currently earning $50,000 per year as a resident physician, however he'll be finishing his residency in one year, at which time he'll earn his full salary, which will be above six figures. As his parents helped him out by paying for his education, he has no student loan and no other debt.

Considering the above situation, it's pretty clear that Joe is in a transition period in his life. Once he's making his full salary, he would easily be able to pay off the $15,000 owing on his line of credit, and he'll have saved $32,000 by purchasing the home a year earlier.

The above is just an example to demonstrate that there are times when it may make sense to purchase a home using borrowed funds.

If you choose to borrow funds for the down payment, it has to be from a source that has a verifiable payment structure such as a line of credit. Money borrowed from friends or family is not acceptable as the repayment structure for the loan can't be confirmed.

KEEP SOME MONEY ASIDE

If you end up choosing to put down the maximum your financial situation will allow, I always recommend holding back at least a bit of it. Some people will have resources to put down 40% for example, and will put every single penny they have into their home, draining all their savings right down to near zero balances.

Always factor in for additional expenses you may incur after taking possession. Unless you are okay with using old milk crates and the cardboard boxes from your move as temporary furniture, then you may want to hold something back. This way, you can furnish your home the way you really want to.

Other things you may need to purchase following closing:

- Window coverings (particularly if it's a new build.) Unless you like the idea of feeling like you're in a fishbowl where your neighbors can watch your every move, you'll likely want to cover up.
- Lawn mower. Unless you want your neighbors to think they're living beside the Clampett's, you'll need a mower. Alternatively, you could always just buy a goat.

- Cookware. Moving into a new home may mean you'll want to upgrade some of your old cookware. Continuing to use the old frying pan your mom gave you when you first moved out may not cut it for the new home.
- Towels. You are moving into your new home! Time to cut up your old towels and use them as cleaning rags. Enjoy the new home experience to the fullest and buy yourself some new towels to go with it.

You won't have a full idea of what exactly you'll need until you've moved in. You also have no way of knowing if you're only a month away from your air conditioner or fridge conking out. Repairs and maintenance can be a costly part of home ownership, so you'll want to ensure you have some funds to pay for certain things as they occur.

Once you've gotten a feel for your new place and are content that you have everything you need, you can then always put that extra money back into your mortgage using your prepayment privileges. I'll be talking more about using prepayment privileges in Chapter Seven.

CHAPTER SIX HIGHLIGHTS

- Minimum down payment to purchase a home is 5%.
- Homes over $500,000 will require 5% of the first $500,000 and 10% on the amount over $500,000.
- Homes over $1 million require 20% down payment.
- 20% is the minimum down payment needed to avoid mortgage default insurance.
- Always look at how fast homes are appreciating in your area and compare that with how long it would take you to save up 20% down payment. It may be cheaper to pay the insurance premium incurred from a lower down payment.
- Homes in the GTA have appreciated every year from 1997 through to the time of writing in early 2017.
- What is your purpose for purchasing a home? Are you looking for an investment or are you looking for a home for your family to live in?
- Speak with a financial advisor before putting all your money into your down payment.
- Keep some money aside for miscellaneous expenses or purchases that may arise after closing.

Just as with the choice between fixed and variable, the best amount to use for down payment is a personal decision. It comes down to what you feel most comfortable with. Take the time to carefully outline your options and write out the benefits to each option. Take the time to speak with a financial advisor and then do what you think will be best suited to you and your family.

CHAPTER SEVEN

SECRETS TO SAVING ON YOUR MORTGAGE

D AVE AND TAMARA, A YOUNG couple in their mid-twenties, were very excited when they purchased their first home. A one bedroom condo in the heart of downtown Toronto. After speaking with their bank, they signed for a 5 year fixed mortgage. They did some research and most of their friends have 5 year fixed mortgages as well, so it seemed like the right product for them. They also figured they would be in the condo for at least 5 years as they loved the area.

However, after living in the condo for two years, Tamara gave birth to their first child. They then realized that the small 600 sq. ft. condo was far too small for their new family, so they purchased a new home and were shocked that the penalty to break their mortgage was close to $10,000.

UNDERSTAND YOUR NEEDS

Back in Chapter Two, I talked about choosing the right mortgage for you. It can be pretty hard to predict where life is going to take you in the next 5 years, but there are definitely signs you can look for. Single people should always think twice before committing to a 5 year fixed for example. Choosing the wrong product can be extremely costly, as was the case with Dave and Tamara above.

Always consider possibilities for the future and think clearly about your specific situation. Some of the questions you can ask yourself are as follows:

- Could there be a change in my relationship status?
- Possibility of having kids over the next few years?
- Is it possible my employment could require me to move?
- Am I planning on staying within the province?

In these cases, you may want to consider going with a shorter term, which would typically come with a lower rate than the traditional 5 year fixed. You can also use the lower payment as leverage to accelerating the pay off of your mortgage, which I'll be discussing later in this chapter.

HOW TO GET THE BEST DEAL

It definitely doesn't hurt to call a few banks or brokers to find out if you are getting a competitive rate. It's amazing how many people don't take the time to simply send out a few emails or make a couple of phone calls. Sometimes there can be a difference in rate as high as 30 basis points[1] from one lender to another.

So how does this translate into real numbers?

Let's say you have a $300,000 mortgage amortized over 30 years. Lender A is offering a 5 year fixed rate of 2.89% while lender B is offering 2.59%. The savings for lender B works out to $4,491.72 over the 5 year term.[2] This is money that could be in your pocket as opposed to the banks.

Back in Chapter Four, I gave you a list of questions to ask your broker and one of them was to determine exactly how many different lenders that broker deals with. If they are putting their business predominantly with a single lender, then there is a good chance they may not be getting you the best available rate. Not every broker has access to every lender. A broker very well may be giving the lowest rate they are able to, however lower rates might be available through another lender that they aren't familiar with.

---

1 Basis points (abbreviated as BPS) are fractions of 1%. For example, 1 basis point is equivalent to 0.01%.

2 Total savings is calculated by using the payment from the higher rate for both options and then calculating the difference in ending balance.

If they are putting their business predominantly with a single lender, then there is a good chance they may not be getting you the best available rate.

The verdict?

Regardless of whether you choose to go with a bank or a broker, speak to at least three different industry professionals so you can get a better handle on what's available. It also doesn't hurt to do a quick Google search, however you can't always believe every rate you see online unfortunately.

WHAT YOUR BANK MAY NOT BE TELLING YOU

In Chapter Three, I discussed how any one specific lender such as a major bank, can only offer their own products. For example, if you walk into BMO, they aren't going to come out and tell you if CIBC happens to have a product that better suits your needs.

Back when I used to work in retail more than twenty years ago, we had a rule of thumb that we had to follow. SWAT. It stood for Sell What's Available Today. If we didn't have an item in stock, we were to push the product that we did have available at that time, which would increase our chances of making the sale on that day. Banks are going to employ a similar system to SWAT by only selling the products they have available to them.

Makes sense of course, right?

Why would TD try to sell you Scotiabank's products? They wouldn't. As they are only going to sell their own products, they may not be so quick to tell you about any potential disadvantages to their products, as they know telling you may result in you going elsewhere for your mortgage.

STANDARD CHARGE VS. COLLATERAL CHARGE MORTGAGE

A mortgage is really just an amortized[1] loan secured by collateral on real estate. As your home is secured as collateral, the lender is able to offer you a lower rate than they could if the loan were unsecured (no collateral). Should the borrower default on the mortgage, the lender has rights associated with the property it was secured against.

The mortgage gets secured to the property with what's called a charge, which is similar to a lien. There are two types of charges that can be used.

Standard charge or collateral charge.

Standard Charge

With a standard charge mortgage, you can switch to a different lender at the end of your term with all legal and appraisal costs covered for you. This is referred to as a switch or a transfer. The only cost you would incur is the discharge fee from your current lender, which is typically around $300. This discharge fee gets added to your new mortgage amount. Some lenders will cover this fee for you, however most of the lower rate lenders will not.

---

1 Amortized meaning that the principal of the loan gradually gets paid down to zero through scheduled payments of principal and interest.

Since the cost is only a few hundred dollars, this can often be made up quite easily with a lower mortgage rate. Most mortgages are registered as a standard charge.

Collateral Charge

Unlike a standard charge, a collateral mortgage typically can't be switched with costs covered for you at the end of your term. This means changing lenders would involve a refinance, which is a slightly different type of transaction. With a refinance, you'll also have to pay legal fees to register a new mortgage, and quite likely, appraisal costs as well. That's in addition to your discharge fee. Total estimated costs can be anywhere from around $800 to $1,400.

With new mortgage regulations announced back in October of 2016, refinances are now more costly for lenders than they are with insurable[1] purchases and switches. For this reason, refinancing can be as much as 30 basis points[2] higher than a straight switch, which can add to the cost of a collateral mortgage significantly.

Refinancing can be as much as 30 basis points higher than a straight switch

---

1   Refer to the section entitled "The New Age of Mortgages" in Chapter One for more information on the difference between insurable and uninsurable mortgages.

2   A basis point is equal to 0.01%.

Let's use a 5 year fixed rate of 2.69% on a switch and 2.99% on a refinance as an example. On a $400,000 mortgage amortized over 25 years, the difference works out to $5,935.03.[1] This may seriously limit your options at maturity, which may make switching to a different lender cost prohibitive.

These are the only disadvantages to having a collateral mortgage, but as you can tell, it's definitely something that needs to be taken into consideration before signing the mortgage papers.

The benefit to a collateral mortgage is that it can make it easier to borrow additional funds in the future IF you choose to register the mortgage for more than it's face value (mortgage amount).

For example, if your home is worth $400,000 and your required mortgage is $320,000, you can choose to register the mortgage for the full $400,000 value (or even higher in some cases). This would allow you to borrow additional funds against your home as it appreciates.

Because your home is already registered at a higher amount, there is no need to register additional security, therefore there would be no legal fees involved in doing so. Otherwise, it would cost around $1,000 to obtain this secondary financing.

Sounds okay, right?

Well, the problem is that you still need to qualify for that additional financing. If the bank says no then you are out of luck and have no other options as the bank has already tied up all your equity (I recently had a client in this same situation). If you do qualify, then great, you 'potentially' saved yourself about $1,000 in set up costs. However.... at the end of your term, you'll still find it

---

1   When calculating savings on one rate vs. another, the payments need to be made equal to that of the higher rate. The savings is the difference between the balance of each option at the end of the term. By making the payments the same, it compensates for the time value of money, which is the most accurate way to calculate mortgage rate savings.

challenging to switch to a different lender at no cost. This leaves you at the bank's mercy, as they know it will cost you money to leave them.

Where is their incentive to give you a competitive mortgage rate?

So the options are:

1. Go with a collateral mortgage to save on legal fees 'in case' you choose to borrow additional funds down the road, only to have to pay them later when you switch.

2. Go with a standard charge mortgage and IF you find yourself in a position where you need the additional financing, just pay the legal fee at that time...when you know you need it (and even then, there may be options to avoid it).

With a collateral mortgage, you are paying the legal fee to switch at the end of the term regardless of whether you need additional financing or not. With a standard charge mortgage, you would only pay a legal fee if you needed to borrow additional funds down the road.

All that said, there are some lenders who will cover the refinance fees for you, but it's often at a higher rate than what you would get if you were simply doing a straight switch. Remember, refinances often come at a higher rate. One way or another, you're paying for it.

My verdict?

I see a collateral mortgage benefiting very few borrowers, but it does provide a large benefit to the banks who issue them. It makes it more costly for borrowers to leave them at the end of the term and can therefore help improve their customer retention. I'll be talking more about switching at the end of your term vs. staying with your current lender later in this chapter.

Zero Benefit Collateral Mortgages

As already mentioned, the only way to see any benefit from a collateral mortgage is if you choose to register the mortgage for a higher amount than what's actually needed. However, most collateral mortgages end up getting registered only for the face value of the mortgage. In other words, the amount borrowed. This is because there are a few lenders who register ALL their new mortgages as collateral, regardless of whether you choose to register the mortgage for a higher amount or not. At the time of writing, these lenders are TD, National Bank and Tangerine.

Other Collateral Mortgages

I mentioned that TD, National Bank and Tangerine register all their mortgages as collateral, however it's possible to have a collateral mortgage with other lenders as well.

Any mortgage having more than one component to it will also be collateral. It doesn't matter if your lender is TD, CIBC, MCAP, First National, or whoever. If it has more than one component, then it will be a collateral charge. Period. This means if you are registering a HELOC (Home Equity Line Of Credit) together with your mortgage as a single charge, then the mortgage registration will be collateral.

Any mortgage having more than one component to it will also be collateral.

The same principal applies to any other multi-component or hybrid mortgages. Sometimes banks will offer to break your mortgage up into multiple components. Let's say you need to borrow $450,000. They may suggest $225,000 fixed and $225,000 variable. The numbers don't have to be even and can be any combination as long as they total the mortgage amount needed. For example, it can be $100,000 fixed and $350,000 variable, it doesn't matter. They may also offer half as a 2 year fixed and the other half as a 5 year fixed… or any combination of mortgage products.

Any mortgage with this type of set up would be registered as a collateral charge, so always think carefully if this type of mortgage is presented to you. Personally… I really fail to see any point in setting up your mortgage this way, however banks will periodically offer these options to their clients.

Conventional vs. Collateral

As a mortgage broker, I frequently have clients asking if the mortgage product I suggest for them is a conventional mortgage. It's very common for people to refer to a non-collateral mortgage as 'conventional', but this terminology can lead you to the wrong information. A conventional mortgage is something different entirely.

It's very common for people to refer to a non-collateral mortgage as 'conventional', but this terminology can lead you to the wrong information.

So what is a conventional mortgage?

The definition of a conventional mortgage was detailed in the first chapter, however it's worth repeating here. Any mortgage with 20% or greater equity (or a purchase with a down payment of 20% or greater) is considered a conventional mortgage, regardless of the type of charge.

Let's say you walk into TD for example. You tell them that you have 20% down and that you want to make sure they are giving you a conventional mortgage. They can assure you with confidence that you will in fact be getting a conventional mortgage. However, they may not tell you that this conventional mortgage will also be registered as a collateral charge. They aren't misleading you here either. They are simply answering your question... and answering it correctly.

If you want to ask about the type of charge then ask if it's a standard charge mortgage. Or even better, ask flat out if its a collateral mortgage, just to ensure there is no confusion. Even in these cases, I've had multiple clients present this question to their bank, and were told flat out that their mortgage is not collateral, only for them to find out later that it was.

This is why it's always a good idea to ask a lot of questions as I outlined in Chapter Four. Get an idea of that individual's experience level so you know you're getting the right answers. In the end, if you're getting a new mortgage with TD, National Bank or Tangerine, then your mortgage will definitely be a collateral charge. The only exception to this is if you are switching in from another lender at the end of your term. Switching means transferring your current balance over from another lender without increasing the amortization or mortgage amount.

UNDERSTANDING MORTGAGE PENALTIES

Regardless of whether you are in a fixed or variable rate mortgage, all closed mortgages carry a penalty if you find yourself in a position where you need to break it early. As explained in Chapter One, most mortgages in Canada are closed. The opposite is an open mortgage, which doesn't have a penalty associated with breaking it early. Rates on open mortgages are significantly higher, making them cost prohibitive in most cases.

Variable Rate Penalties

Variable rate mortgage penalties are almost always three months interest, regardless of the lender you are dealing with. Most of which will use the contract rate to calculate the penalty (the rate your payment is based on). Some however, may use prime rate, which would result in a slightly higher penalty. It's best to ask your broker or the bank to confirm which rate your penalty is based on.

There are however, some exceptions to the standard three months interest penalty. There are a few variable products that come with a substantially higher penalty, typically around 2.75 or 3.00% of the balance. When breaking a mortgage at 2.25% with a $300,000 balance, the three months interest penalty would be $1,687. At 2.75%, the penalty would be $8,250. Huge difference.

So why would anyone go with a variable rate that comes with such a high break penalty?

Most of the time, these products are at lower rates, which make them seem more attractive. Many borrowers end up choosing these options for this reason, thinking they will save money.

After all, if you don't plan on breaking your mortgage over the next five years, then why not go with the lower rate?

Many people say they have no intention of breaking their mortgage, yet so many people do. I spoke about this in detail back in Chapter One in the section on 10 year mortgages. The problem is that circumstances change. Things come up. Life throws you curveballs. Anything can happen in a five year period. As a result, a large number of borrowers end up breaking their mortgages before the end of five years. If many of these people knew they would be breaking before the end of their term, they would have taken a shorter term to begin with. Providing these options were presented to them of course, and that they weren't pushed into a longer term by an unscrupulous broker or bank specialist.

A large number of borrowers end up breaking their mortgages before the end of five years

To justify going with a variable with a high break fee, I like to see at least a 10 point discount on rate. There also must be a reasonable certainty that the borrower will be content with this home for the full 5 year term. Even then, it doesn't come without strong warning.

An example of this would be a couple who has been married for 10+ years with a great relationship and no plans to ever move out of their home. The opposite would be a couple in their twenties that have been dating for 6 months who are purchasing their first home. See the difference?

Fixed Mortgage Penalties

While the penalty on the variable rate is typically just three months, the penalties to break a fixed rate mortgage are more complicated. Regardless of which lender you go with, the penalty to break most fixed rate mortgages will be the <u>higher</u> of three months interest or the interest rate differential (IRD).

The IRD is the difference between your current mortgage rate and the rate offered by the lender at the time you break your mortgage. The differential refers to the difference between the two rates, which is the basic definition. However, the wording varies from lender to lender. Three months interest is three months interest. But when it comes to the IRD, all penalties are not created equal. The IRD has multiple different ways of calculating it, and each way can provide a substantially different figure.

If you have a 5 year term on your mortgage, then you have a contract for five years. By breaking the mortgage, you are breaking the contract. The idea behind the concept of the IRD is to compensate the lender for lost profits incurred when re-lending the funds.

Let's say for example you have a 5 year fixed at 2.99% and choose to break it after three years. The rate at the time is 2.69%. This means the lender will be getting 0.30% less interest when they re-lend out the money you are paying back. The IRD compensates them for this loss.

Interest Rate Differential (IRD) Calculation Methods

There are three different ways lenders calculate the IRD:

1. Based on the contract rate (the rate you are paying on your mortgage). This is the best and most fair way for a lender to calculate the IRD penalty. This is the method used by lenders such as Street Capital, First National, Merix, and most other monoline lenders.
2. Based on a reinvestment rate. This is a rate that is often lower than the rate at the time you break your mortgage, which can result in a higher penalty. This is the preferred method by lenders such as Industrial Alliance.
3. Based on the posted rate. This is the method that all the big banks use. Because they are basing their IRD penalty on a much higher rate, the result will be an inflated penalty.

So the lenders with the lowest IRD penalties would be the ones using the first method. If their rates are higher at the time you would break your mortgage, then the IRD penalty would most likely not be a factor. With the other two methods however, you'll still likely pay the IRD, even if their rates at the time are higher than the rate you are paying.

BREAKING YOUR MORTGAGE MID-TERM

There are a few reasons why people would break mid-term, many of which we have previously discussed. Often, it's because you are selling your house and buying another one. In this case, you can typically port your mortgage over to the new property and do a blended mortgage on the increase. This means you would transfer your current balance over to the new property. You would continue to pay the current rate on the amount owing, and for the increase in funds needed, you would pay the rate offered by your lender at that time. These two payments would then be blended together giving you a single rate and payment for the new term. This is what is referred to as a blended mortgage.

There is no penalty involved when porting a mortgage.

Porting however, usually only works out well with fixed rate mortgages. While variable rate mortgages are typically portable, most lenders will only let you port over the current balance. No increase in funds or blended mortgage would be available. Since most people need to borrow additional funds in these cases, your only option would be to break the mortgage and pay the penalty.

While variable rate mortgages are typically portable, most lenders will only let you port over the current balance.

Regardless of fixed or variable, it still may make sense to pay the penalty as opposed to porting. It all depends on what's being offered at the time compared with how much your penalty would be to break your current mortgage. In the end, the numbers will guide you in the right direction and a good broker or bank mortgage specialist can help you determine your best course of action.

Refinancing

Another reason for breaking your mortgage early would be to refinance.

There are two main reasons for refinancing:

A) To get a lower interest rate. This would involve breaking your mortgage and paying a penalty, regardless of whether you transfer to a new lender or stay with your current one.

B) To draw equity out of the home if you need money for any reason. If you find yourself in a situation like this, you can usually refinance with the same lender at zero penalty, as they would just do a blended mortgage as described above. Lenders like Industrial Alliance may have a higher penalty, but they almost always have super competitive rates. Therefore, you shouldn't have to worry about being offered a rate that isn't competitive on the increased funds. Just as with porting, it doesn't always make sense to stay with the same lender. Sometimes you can find greater savings by breaking the mortgage and paying the penalty. It all comes down to what your lender is offering you compared with what else is being offered at the time.

LEVERAGE YOUR PREPAYMENT PRIVILEGES

All mortgages will have some sort of prepayment privilege allowing you to pay your mortgage off faster without incurring a penalty. Any money paid over and above your scheduled payments will get applied 100% to principal, regardless of the lender you are dealing with. The principle is always the same without exception.

There are two components to prepayment privileges:

1. Increase payment
2. Lump sum payments

Prepayment privileges can range from 5% to 20%. They are typically written as 15/15 or 20/20. These numbers are always equal to each other and it would be unusual to see 10/20 for example.

This means that with 15/15 prepayment privileges you can increase your payments by up to 15%, or you can pay up to 15% of the original mortgage balance as a lump sum payment. This is over and above your scheduled payments. With most lenders, you can do a combination of each, providing you don't exceed the lump sum maximum.

For example, if you have a $300,000 mortgage with 15/15 prepayment privileges, you will be able to pay up to $45,000 per year toward your mortgage in addition to your regular mortgage payments. If you were to prepay this entire amount then you would not be able to increase your payments by 15% as well. This is the case with most lenders, however there are lenders who will allow you to fully utilize both, however they are few and far between.

Increasing Your Payments

When increasing your payment, the privileges are cumulative. If you have 15% prepayment privileges, you're permitted to increase by an additional 15% each year based on the already increased payment.

For example, let's say your monthly payment is $1,000. If you max out the increase in the first year, your payment would then be $1,150. You can then increase the $1,150 by another 15% the following year, and so on. The payment structure would look like this:

Year 1-$1,150
Year 2-$1,322.50
Year 3-$1,520.88
Year 4-$1,749.01
Year 5-$2,011.36

This is how it works with most mortgage lenders. Some lenders however will only let you increase each year based on the original payment amount. In which case, the structure would look like this:

Year 1-$1,150
Year 2-$1,300
Year 3-$1,450
Year 4-$1,600
Year 5-$1750

The above structure can only be followed if you're increasing your payments each year. For example, you can't go from your original payment all the way up to a payment of $2,011.36 in your 5th year if you were not already increasing the payments each year previously.

Most lenders will allow you to revert back to your original payment at any time during your term should you need to increase your cash flow. Never assume this however, and always double check, as there are a few lenders where you won't be able to lower your payment after increasing it.

Making Lump Sum Payments

Some lenders limit to how many times you can make lump sum payments. With some you are only limited to a single time per year, while others may allow you up to three times per year. Most however will let you make as many lump sum payments as you like, providing they fall on a scheduled payment date and that you don't exceed the maximum annual limit.

Let's say for example you have a mortgage with an original balance of $400,000, amortized over 30 years at 2.99% with monthly payments and 20/20 prepayment privileges. Your lender allows you to make as many lump sum payments as you like, providing they fall on a scheduled payment date.

This would allow you to pay $80,000 towards your mortgage each year in addition to your regular payments. As your mortgage has monthly payments, you will have twelve payments per year, which means you could increase each payment by an additional $6666.67, which would go straight to your principal. When added to your regular monthly payment of $1,680.28, you'd be paying $8,346.95 per month.

This would result in an effective amortization of only 4 years, 3 months, and a few days. In other words, your mortgage would be paid off in its entirety in only 4 years, 3 months, and a few days. The original amortization is meaningless.

Paying an additional $80,000 per year toward their mortgage is not an option for the vast majority of homeowners, but it gives you an example of what's possible.

Now let's take a look at a scenario that is a little more realistic. Using the same mortgage above, let's say you choose to make an additional lump sum payment of $5,000 once per year on the anniversary date.

This strategy would drop your amortization down to 27 years, 4 months and would give you a projected savings of $28,654.82 in interest over the years. This is based on the first 5 years alone. If you were to carry this strategy on throughout the life of your mortgage, the amount of savings would increase significantly.

Do you plan on using your prepayment privileges?

Some products might have more limited prepayment privileges such as 5/5, which are offered at a lower rate as a result. If you aren't going to use your prepayment privileges, then why pay extra for them? Keep in mind that on a $400,000 mortgage, 5% prepayment privileges still allows you to pay an additional $20,000 per year over and above your regular payments. More than most will ever use. This 5% prepayment option is not too common in our industry, but it does exist. One lender that always has it available is Industrial Alliance and it's only available on mortgages closing within 30 days.

LEVERAGING YOUR PAYMENTS WITH VARIABLE RATE MORTGAGES

One strategy I often give to my clients who are interested in both fixed and variable is to go with a variable, but then set your payment as if you had chosen the higher fixed rate.

For example, let's say you need to borrow $450,000 amortized over 30 years. The two options you are most interested in are a 5 year variable at 2.50% or a 5 year fixed at 2.99%.

If going variable, your monthly payment would be $1,775.02.

If going fixed, your monthly payment would be $1,890.32

Since you're contemplating the higher payment anyway, and you're comfortable paying this amount, why not consider going with the variable option, but increase your payments to match the payment on the 5 year fixed rate? The additional funds of course go straight to principal. Using this strategy alone, you would save $10,988.68 over the next 5 years. Assuming no change to the variable rate of course. This strategy would fall within the limits of most prepayment allowances as the increase to payment is only around 6.5%, so if you had an allowance of 20% increase to payment, you could still increase your payment by another 13.5% and still be within your limits.

Why not consider going with the variable option, but increase your payments to match the payment on the 5 year fixed rate?

MORTGAGE RATE INFLATION HEDGE STRATEGY

One of the most common questions I get from my clients is where I see interest rates going in the next few years. Usually from the ones who are still unsure as to which term they are looking for or whether to choose fixed or variable. If it's being predicted that rates will stay low over the next few years, then the client might opt for a shorter term or variable rate product to save some money on a lower rate. If it looks as though rates could be increasing they'll want to lock in for a longer fixed term.

The truth is, no one knows for sure what's going to happen with rates. All we can do is speculate. In other words... we're guessing. Even Canada's top economists, who are paid large sums of money for their opinions, often get it wrong. At the time of writing in early 2017, we are currently in one of the longest streaks in history where we have not had an increase to prime rate. From 2011 through to 2014, I've heard economists predicting that we will see an increase to prime rate 'next year'.

What eventually happened?

Prime rate dropped early in 2015. Twice.

The only way to know for sure where rates are heading is to get yourself a good quality, sparkling crystal ball. (Mine is currently being professionally polished).

Since no one can be certain, the following hedge strategy can be implemented. Not to protect yourself from rising rates. There is no way to do that. But you can strategize to make rising rates much more painless for you. I'm talking about hedging against potentially increasing mortgage rates.

What is a hedge?

I'm not talking about a row of small shrubs (although planting some may help with your resale). A hedge is a way of protecting yourself against financial loss. In this case, the idea is to get a head start against rising rates by artificially increasing them yourself.

Huh?

Let me better explain.

All you're doing is using your prepayment privileges to increase your payment to match that of a higher rate, starting right from the beginning of your mortgage. You then increase it again in the second, third, fourth, and fifth year. As your income increases from year to year, you simply increase your mortgage payment. This way, when rates do start to increase, you're already making payments based on a higher rate. Although, the additional payments you have been making are going straight to your principal as opposed to paying interest at a higher rate. By the time rates increase, you'll have already paid your mortgage down further. This means the higher rate will be calculated on a lower balance, which will result in you paying less interest.

This works equally well for both fixed and variable rates.

Hedge strategy with fixed rates

Let's take a look at an example to give you a better idea of what I'm talking about by examining the following mortgage:

Mortgage amount-$300,000
Amortization – 25 years
Rate – 2.89%
Term-5 year fixed
Monthly payment-$1,402.86

Now let's make a prediction that the 5 year fixed rate will be 3.99% at the end of 5 years. We of course have no way of knowing for sure what it will be and all we can do is guess. Without making any additional payments and maintaining your regular monthly payment schedule throughout the term, at the end of 5 years you'll owe $255,879.53.

If you were to renew for another 5 years, the new mortgage would look like this:

Mortgage amount: $255,879.53
Amortization – 20 years
Rate-3.99%
Term – 5 year fixed
Monthly payment-$1,544.82

This represents a payment increase of $141.96 over what you were used to paying with your first term, which can be fairly significant for many people.

So here's where the fun begins!

Since we're using a 5 year term in this example, we are going to divide the future payment increase by five and then increase the mortgage payment by that amount. This works out to be an increase of $28.39 per year. You can handle that, can't you?

So here's what the payment structure would look like along with the ending balance each year when implementing the $28.39 increase right from the very first payment.

	Payment Amount	Mortgage Balance
Year 1	$1,431.25	$291,329.68
Year 2	$1,459.64	$282,061.79
Year 3	$1,488.03	$272,178.91
Year 4	$1,516.42	$261,663.16
Year 5	$1,544.81	$250,496.10

At the end of 5 years, you'll be used to paying the equivalent of a 3.99% rate, which will remove the shock of having such a large payment increase as result. This scenario represents an interest savings of $273.23 at the end of 5 years. Now, $273 may not exactly get your birds chirping, but it's still $273 that you won't have to pay to the bank. You will also have eliminated the shock of having to make a higher payment if the rates did increase to this level.

If your rate remained unchanged until the mortgage was paid to zero, and you maintained the $1,544.81 payment, you would save a total of $14,143.87. That being said, no change in rate is a pretty big assumption! The odds of your interest rate remaining unchanged throughout the life of your mortgage is about the same as Paris Hilton winning an Oscar for best actress. It's just not going to happen. But I thought I'd include this example for anyone who may be interested in the 'but what if' scenario. Plus, it's fun to dream!

This will also shorten your effective amortization from 25 years down to 22 years, 1.5 months based on the first five years alone. Following this simple strategy, at the end of five years your ending balance will be $5,383.43 lower than it would have been if you just stuck with your regular scheduled payments. This means that at the end of your term, you may be paying a higher rate, but it will be on a lower balance.

Here's how it would look if your rate actually did increase to 3.99% at the end of your term. If you had implemented the hedge strategy, the new mortgage at renewal would look like this:

Mortgage amount: $250,496.10
Amortization – 20 years (Based on it being 5 years later)
Rate-3.99%
Term – 5 year fixed
Monthly payment-$1,512.32

The first thing you may notice is that the monthly payment is lower than the $1,544.82 we used for the hedge strategy. As the balance was lowered from increasing your payments, the payment at the start of the new term is also lower as a result. The payment used in the hedge strategy was based on you not taking any action at all. As you've implemented the hedge strategy, you now have a lower payment on your new term.

You can then implement the strategy again for the next 5 years and carry it out straight through until the mortgage is paid off to zero. If the opposite were to happen and rates were to decrease, then you'll be all that much further ahead of the game and you could potentially save thousands!

Hedge strategy with variable rates

This strategy also works great for variable rate mortgages. It can be a great technique for those who are intrigued by variable rates, but are still sitting on the fence as to whether or not variable might be right for them. The biggest concern with variable rate mortgages is that your rate and payment can start increasing at any time. For this reason, many people choose to go fixed, which is also a completely fine option. The choice really depends on two things:

1. The spread between fixed and variable
2. Your risk threshold

The spread between fixed and variable is the difference between the two rates at the time you are arranging your mortgage. For example, if you are offered a fixed rate at 3.00% and a variable at 2.50%, then the spread is 0.50%. Variable is based on prime rate, so when the prime rate increases, so does your rate and payment. The thinner the spread, the more risky a variable rate mortgage becomes. When prime rate moves, it typically changes by 0.25%. This means if you have a spread of 0.50%, then two rate increases by the Bank of Canada would make your variable equal to where fixed would have been, had you gone in that direction.

When prime rate moves, it typically changes by 0.25%.

If the spread was even thinner at 0.25%, then risk would be increased since it would only take a single rate increase for the rates to become equal. Two rate increases would send your variable rate higher than the alternative fixed option. If we look at the period between 2006 up to the time of writing in early 2017, only once has the prime rate moved by 0.50%.

For some people, the thought of their rate and payment changing at any time can be very scary. They need reassurance that everything will stay the same for the entire term, and for this reason they choose a fixed rate. As mentioned in Chapter Two, variable rate mortgages are not for people who are risk averse. There are however always people sitting on the fence and are still unsure whether they should go fixed or variable. Applying the mortgage hedge strategy in this case can help make the decision easier.

To illustrate the inflation hedge strategy on a variable rate, we'll use different numbers from the fixed example, just to keep things fun. Just like with the strategy used for fixed rates, we will be artificially increasing the variable rate as well.

We'll use the following mortgage for our example:

Mortgage amount-$425,000
Amortization – 30 years
Rate – 2.15%
Term-5 year variable
Payment-$1,600.90 (scheduled monthly payment)

Let's assume that the prime rate will be increasing by 0.50% each year for the next 5 years. In other words, two increases per year. We really have no clue of course whether or not this will actually happen, but the entire purpose of this strategy is not to try to accurately predict the future. It's to prepare for the unforeseen so you can be better prepared for future payment shock. If it does in fact happen, then you'll already be used to making the higher payment. If it doesn't end up happening and if prime rate remains unchanged, or drops over the next 5 years, then all that extra money you paid will have gone straight to your principal. In either case, you're a winner.

There are of course a million potential scenarios that could be taken into consideration. We'll however keep things simple by analyzing just three of them. I'll leave the other 999,997 up to you. Everything is speculation of course and anything can happen. The main purpose of this strategy is to help protect you against the shock of suddenly increasing payments in an environment where prime rate is steadily increasing.

The main purpose of this strategy is to help protect you against the shock of suddenly increasing payments in an environment where prime rate is steadily increasing.

The first scenario is how your payment structure would look if you maintained your scheduled payments without increasing them and assuming no change to prime rate over the term.

	Rate	Payment amount	Mortgage Balance
Year 1	2.15	$1,600.90	$414,786.23
Year 2	2.15	$1,600.90	$404,351.69
Year 3	2.15	$1,600.90	$393,691.60
Year 4	2.15	$1,600.90	$382,801.08
Year 5	2.15	$1,600.90	$371,675.15

This gives you an idea of how everything looks on paper before we even start getting our hands dirty.

Now it's time to start the fun stuff!

The second scenario will also assume no change to prime rate, but will implement the hedge strategy by increasing the payment to match a rate increase of 0.50% per year starting in year two.

	Rate	Payment amount	Mortgage Balance
Year 1	2.15	$1,600.90	$414,786.23
Year 2	2.65	$1,706.11	$403,076.69
Year 3	3.15	$1,811.67	$389,834.25
Year 4	3.65	$1,917.25	$375,026.68
Year 5	4.15	$2,022.55	$358,622.98

At the end of 5 years, you'll be used to making payments based on a rate of 4.15%, which will remove future payment shock should such rates increase to this level. This scenario represents a savings of $403.78 at the end of 5 years and leaves you with only 17.77 years remaining after the first 5 years. Not too bad considering you started out with a 30 year amortization on paper.

That means your balance at the end of your term would be $13,052 less than it would have been had you maintained your regular payment schedule.

The third scenario demonstrates what the numbers would look like if this situation actually panned out and your rate actually did increase by the 0.50% each year. For simplicity, I've implemented the 0.50% rate increase at the start of each year.

	Rate	Payment amount	Mortgage Balance
Year 1	2.15	$1,600.90	$414,786.23
Year 2	2.65	$1,706.11	$405,128.44
Year 3	3.15	$1,811.67	$395,935.88
Year 4	3.65	$1,917.25	$387,126.55
Year 5	4.15	$2,022.55	$378,625.41

This gives you an idea of how things would look if our hypothetical rate increasing rampage became reality. Your payment increases would have amounted to an additional $12,647.76, while your ending balance would be $378,625.41 instead of $371,675.15 had you maintained your initial payment and rate had remained the same. So in other words, you've paid out an additional $12,647.76, yet your ending balance increased by $6,950.26. Add the two together, and these rate increases have cost you an additional $19,598.02 over the 5 year term. This is exactly why utilizing your prepayment privileges can be a wise decision. This way, when rates start to increase, you'll be paying the higher rate on a lower balance and will therefore be paying less interest.

MANIPULATING AMORTIZATION WITH PREPAYMENT PRIVILEGES

The definition of amortization is the amount of time it would take to pay your mortgage down to zero while maintaining equal payments. This means that as soon as you increase your payment or make any sort of lump sum payment towards your mortgage, your amortization drops. In a sense, the original amortization becomes completely irrelevant in this case.

When maintaining your scheduled payments, the amount of interest you pay decreases with every payment, while the amount that goes towards principal increases with each payment.

To demonstrate how a mortgage is paid down without using the prepayment privileges, we'll use a $400,000 mortgage at 2.99%, amortized over 30 years as an example. The monthly payment would be $1,680.28, and just to be wild and crazy, let's start the payments on March 1st. The breakdown of each payment for the first year would look like this:

Pmt Date	Interest	Principal	Total Pmt	Balance
March 1st	$990.51	$689.77	$1,680.28	$399,310.23
April 1st	$988.81	$691.47	$1,680.28	$398,618.76
May 1st	$987.09	$693.19	$1,680.28	$396,534.05
June 1st	$985.38	$694.90	$1,680.28	$397,230.67
July 1st	$983.66	$696.62	$1,680.28	$396,534.05
Aug 1st	$981.93	$698.35	$1,680.28	$395,835.70
Sept 1st	$980.20	$700.08	$1,680.28	$395,135.62
Oct 1st	$978.47	$701.81	$1,680.28	$394,433.81
Nov 1st	$976.73	$703.55	$1,680.28	$393,730.26
Dec. 1st	$974.99	$705.29	$1,680.28	$393,024.97
Jan 1st	$973.24	$707.04	$1,680.28	$392,317.93
Feb 1st	$971.49	$708.79	$1,680.28	$391,609.14

As you can see, the amount of your payment that goes towards principal increases with each and every payment, while the amount paid towards interest decreases. In this case, the amount going to principal increases by approximately $1.70 each month and then continues to increase a penny or so every couple of months. This also of course means you're paying $1.70 less towards interest with each and every payment.

Now let's take the same mortgage, but we'll increase the payments by 15%.

Pmt Date	Interest	Principal	Total Pmt	Balance
March 1st	$990.51	$941.81	$1,932.32	$399,058.19
April 1st	$988.18	$944.14	$1,932.32	$398,114.05
May 1st	$985.84	$946.48	$1,932.32	$397,167.57
June 1st	$983.50	$948.82	$1,932.32	$396,218.75
July 1st	$981.15	$951.17	$1,932.32	$395,267.58
Aug 1st	$978.80	$953.52	$1,932.32	$394,314.06
Sept 1st	$976.43	$955.89	$1,932.32	$393,358.17
Oct 1st	$974.07	$958.25	$1,932.32	$392,399.92
Nov 1st	$971.69	$960.63	$1,932.32	$391,439.29
Dec. 1st	$969.32	$963.00	$1,932.32	$390,476.29
Jan 1st	$966.93	$965.39	$1,932.32	$389,510.90
Feb 1st	$964.54	$967.78	$1,932.32	$388,543.12

The portion of your payment going to principal jumps from $1.70 to $2.33 from your very first payment. While we are just talking pennies, these pennies start to add up very quickly.

The 15% increase to your payment works out to $252.04 per month or $15,122.40 over the 5 year term. Your ending balance at the end of 5 years would be $16,281.96 less than it would be if you had maintained your regular scheduled payments.

In other words, you paid an additional $15,122.40 toward your mortgage yet the ending balance dropped a total of $16,281.96.

This means you'll come out ahead by $1,159.56 when compared with the regular payment schedule (no increase to payments). By increasing your payments by 15%, you will have also shaved almost 6 years off your projected amortization in the first 5 years alone. Not bad.

Payment Frequency

Most seasoned borrowers have a pretty good grasp on the differences between accelerated biweekly and monthly payments, so this section will be more for the first time homebuyer.

The payment frequency refers to how often your mortgage payment is withdrawn from your account. There are 6 different options:

Monthly
Weekly
Accelerated weekly
Biweekly
Accelerated biweekly
Semi –monthly

Selecting accelerated biweekly over monthly payments will result in a noticeable reduction to your amortization. The amount of the reduction will vary based on interest rate. The higher the rate, the larger the reduction, and vice-versa.

For example, a mortgage at 2.99% with a 30 year amortization would automatically become 26 years, 6 months. If the rate were 3.99%, the effective amortization would drop to 25 years, 11 months.

The amount of the reduction to your amortization will vary based on interest rate. The higher the rate, the larger the reduction, and vice-versa.

The formula for calculating an accelerated biweekly payment is simply the monthly payment divided in half. You would then make that payment every two weeks for a total of 26 payments per year. This works out to the same as making one extra monthly payment per year, which gets applied directly to your principal. That extra monthly payment is spread out evenly over the 26 payments, which makes it much easier to manage. As this results in paying more over traditional monthly payments, it will cut into your cash flow. In situations where money is very tight for you, monthly, semi-monthly, or non-accelerated biweekly payments may be a wiser option. Most lenders will allow you to change your payment frequency at any time during your term without cost.

Most mortgage borrowers in Canada use accelerated biweekly payments compared with the US where most prefer the monthly option.

Accelerated biweekly is not to be confused with regular biweekly, which would be calculated as monthly payment x 12 / 26, which would not reduce your amortization at all.

With accelerated weekly there is negligible benefit over accelerated biweekly, with the additional savings only being about $35 over the full 30 year amortization of a $400,000 mortgage. For accelerated weekly payments, just divide the payment by 4 and multiply by 52. Or for regular weekly, multiply the monthly payment by 12 and divide by 52.

Semi-monthly is just your monthly payment x 12 / 24 with payments are made every two weeks. Semi-monthly over monthly also produces next to zero benefit saving just pennies over the term, as does regular biweekly over monthly.

Which payment frequency is right for you?

The most common is accelerated biweekly. It's an easy way to get your mortgage paid off a little quicker while putting little thought into it. While it does work out to making an additional monthly payment per year, that extra payment spread out over 26 equal payments throughout the year is very manageable for most borrowers.

Some people like to coordinate their mortgage payment with their pay cheques so they both occur on the same date.

As for which is the best option? There is no right or wrong answer here. It comes down to what you feel most comfortable with.

GOING WITH VARIABLE AND SWITCHING TO FIXED MID-TERM

Pretty much every variable rate product offered gives you the option to convert to a fixed rate at any time during the term at no cost. I get clients asking me all the time if I think that going in with this strategy is a good idea.

Going with a variable rate with the expectation of switching to a fixed is rarely a strategy I suggest. The reason is because you can never time the market. It's similar to saying "buy the stock low and sell high and you will make money". Sure, in theory that's correct, but getting the timing right is the challenge. Whenever you decide to convert from variable to fixed, you're agreeing to have an increase in rate and payment beginning with your very next payment. For this reason, people will typically try to hold off for as long as possible until they have a clear indicator that it is time to make the switch. But by this time, it's usually too late. Rates have already increased.

Also, the rate your lender will convert you to would rarely (if ever) be lowest market rate.

At the time of writing, the lowest variable rate is 2.05% with MCAP, so we will use this as an example. If you had this product and wanted to convert to a fixed rate in the middle of your term, the rate they would convert you to would not be today's lowest 5 year fixed of 2.44%. It would be MCAP's regular 5 year fixed rate of 2.69%. Don't expect any sort of deal here.

This is exactly why I suggest staying with your variable rate for the entire term, rather than choosing variable with the intention of switching half way through. Every rule of course has its exception.

WHAT TO EXPECT AT RENEWAL

Your mortgage rate is of course only valid for the length of your term. In other words, a mortgage with a 5 year term would have a rate valid for 5 years. When you reach the end of your mortgage term, your mortgage then becomes due and payable. There are three options for you at this time.

Option 1

You pay the mortgage off in full. Unless you've just won the lottery, this isn't really going to be much of a possibility for most people of course.

Option 2

Renew with your current lender.

Option 3

Switch to a different lender who may have more favourable rates at the time.

As you approach your maturity date, your current lender will send you out a renewal document giving terms of the new rate options for re-signing with them. In most cases, a mortgage is switchable for minimal cost once you reach the end of your term. Providing you don't have a collateral mortgage as described earlier in this chapter, the only fee you would need to pay is your discharge fee from your current lender. The discharge fee usually runs around

$300 and would be added on to your new mortgage. Some lenders will cover this for you, however the rates are often a little higher. In the end, you're usually paying it one way or another.

At this point, you can shop around and see if there may be better deals or rate specials out there. Unfortunately, what many people will do is just sign the renewal document and send it back to the bank. Simply signing the renewal form and sending it back to the lender without doing any research is tantamount to opening up your wallet and emptying it into the trash. Not something any sane person would do. This however is exactly what you are doing when you sign your lender's initial offer at renewal without doing any research on rates.

Simply signing the renewal form and sending it back to the lender without doing any research is tantamount to opening up your wallet and emptying it into the trash

Banks are well aware of this common behavior and will sometimes send you the renewal form with their posted rates. Posted rates are significantly higher than the discounted rates they offer. All you need to do is ask for a lower rate and they will typically oblige. It's really as simple as that. Even then, I wouldn't just accept your banks discounted rate either. At least, not without first doing further research. There are often lower rates to be found. And in many cases... much lower.

For this reason, you'll want to shop around at the end of your mortgage term, which you should start doing around 90 days before your maturity date. This is the maximum amount of time that most lenders will be able to hold a rate for a switch. (For a purchase, the maximum rate hold for discounted rates is 120 days).

A switch usually takes about 3 – 4 weeks to process from time of application through to completion. For this reason, make sure you do all your shopping before hand so you'll be ready to start the process no later than 30 days prior to maturity. This will allow ample time for your bank or broker to get things done for you. Should things run a little late and your maturity date passes without the new mortgage closing, then not to worry in *most* cases. Most lenders will automatically put you into an open mortgage on your maturity date if you have not yet signed with them, or if they have not yet been paid out by another lender.

The rate for an open mortgage is usually much higher than the rate you'll be getting with the new lender. Often a couple percent higher. Keep in mind though that the interest rate is always expressed as an annual basis. In this case, you may only be paying this rate for a few days.

Lets say for example you miss your maturity date by 3 days. The rate you are applying for is a 5 year fixed at 2.79% and your lender's open rate is 4.99%. So really, you're paying an additional 2.20% for those three days over and above the interest you'll be paying on the new mortgage. This extra 2.20% works out to $6,600 in simple interest over the year, but again, you aren't paying this rate for a year. We're only talking about 3 days. $6,600 / 365 days in the year means that the additional cost to you comes to $54.25 for those 3 days, or $18.82 per day. Money is money however, and I'm sure you would still rather avoid paying this extra interest. Just make sure you start setting up your switch early to ensure there is plenty of time to get everything completed by your maturity date.

Remember, I said 'most' lenders will put you into an open mortgage, and this is what happens 99% of the time, but this isn't a given. It's that 1% that you have to be prepared for, just in case. You'll want to confirm this with your lender as some may try to auto-renew you into a closed mortgage. This would mean you would have to pay a stiff penalty to get out of it. For this reason, make sure you contact your lender to find out what their policy is if you miss your maturity date. If they tell you they are going to put you into a closed mortgage, make it clear to them that you want to be renewed into an open mortgage instead.

Make sure you contact your lender to find out what their policy is if you miss your maturity date.

Re-signing with your current lender

While most of the time I suggest shopping for better options at maturity, there are some cases where it makes more sense to re-sign with your current lender. But why?

It's super convenient.
There's no need to re-qualify.
You don't need to provide any documents.
Just simply sign the form and send it in.

The question is… how much is this convenience worth to you? If you could save thousands by switching to a different lender, then why not just provide a few documents and make the switch?

What if you don't qualify?

Life can sometimes throw you curveballs and sometimes bad things happen to good people. There are times when you may find yourself in a situation where you are between jobs, or your credit has taken a hard blow when your maturity date rolls around. If this is the case, then you are likely not going to qualify for a mortgage with another lender. In these situations, signing with your current lender is your best and only option. This however doesn't mean you can't ask them for a lower rate than what they are offering you. Providing you aren't taking out any additional funds, there is no need for them to re-approve you. You're already approved!

This means no credit check.
No employment confirmation.
Nothing.

You could have just lost your job and declared bankruptcy and they aren't going to know about it unless you tell them. This means, you can bluff your way into getting them to offer you a lower rate. Do some shopping around to see what rates are available elsewhere and then ask your current lender if they will match it. Tell them that you've been shopping around and that you can get a much better rate by switching to another lender. You're bluffing of course, as you really don't have any other options, but you'd be surprised how often they will fight for your business. This five-minute phone call alone could save you thousands.

So what if your credit has plummeted and you need to take out additional funds as well? There is hope here as well, which we will discuss in the next chapter.

CHAPTER SEVEN HIGHLIGHTS

- Understand your needs before selecting a mortgage product.
- Talk to at least three different mortgage professionals, banks and brokers, to ensure you're being offered a competitive rate.
- Be aware of mortgages that are registered as collateral charges, as these types of mortgages can be more costly to switch to another lender at the end of your term.
- Penalty calculations to break fixed rate mortgages can vary from lender to lender, with major banks having among the harshest penalty calculations.
- The penalty to break a variable rate mortgage is usually 3 months interest, regardless of the lender. Always ask just to be sure, as there are some exceptions.
- Utilizing your prepayment privileges can save thousands in interest over the life of your mortgage.
- Use the Mortgage Inflation Hedge Strategy to ensure you are prepared for any potential rate increases (and to possibly save yourself thousands at the same time!)
- Never sign your mortgage renewal documents before first shopping around to ensure you are being offered a fair rate.

Carefully selecting your mortgage product and cleverly using your prepayment privileges can help build your equity at a rapid rate. It can also help you to feel a sense of power knowing that you are in control of your mortgage, rather than having it in control of you. No one likes surprises when it comes to their mortgage. Unless of course the bank made an error resulting in you getting a nice, big, fat cash back. Okay, so this doesn't really happen in reality... but we can dream! Make sure you do your research and ask a lot of questions to protect yourself from these surprises down the road. I speak to people regularly that have collateral charge mortgages and they had no idea.

Not everyone is quite as lucky however, and many won't qualify for a traditional mortgage. They are just looking to get approved for a mortgage of any kind. Fortunately, there are alternative lending solutions available, which is what we will be talking about next.

CHAPTER EIGHT

ALTERNATIVE MORTGAGE LENDING

L IFE IS FULL OF UPS and downs and there are times when things can become tough even for the most credit worthy and financially stable individuals. I've dealt with clients who were solid as solid can be when arranging their mortgage. Then, a few years later, they contact me after life threw them a curveball sending their financial situation spiraling downward.

There are a number of things that can cause someone's finances to turn south:

Loss of job
Disability
Divorce
Business venture turned bad
Legal issues

It's unfortunate that bad things sometimes happen to good people, but it happens all the time. It can be next to impossible to get a mortgage through traditional sources when your credit has taken a beating. Fortunately there are alternative lending sources to fill this void.

WHAT IS ALTERNATIVE MORTGAGE LENDING?

An alternative mortgage lender is one that specializes in situations where the applicant does not qualify through an A, or bank type lender. That is, a lender specializing in qualified applicants. Any lender who specializes in mortgages that do not fit within the general parameters of an A lender would be considered an alternative lender.

The following are some of the typical situations that would require alternative lending:

Bad credit
Non-confirmable income*
Non-qualifying income
Refinancing over 80% LTV
Specialty properties

---

* In some cases, non-confirmable income can still be done with an A lender, depending on the situation. See Chapter Five for more information on stated income found in the section on self-employed borrowers.

TYPES OF ALTERNATIVE LENDERS

There are two types of alternative lenders. B lenders and private lenders.

B LENDERS

I discussed the differences between A and B lenders back in Chapter Three, but it's definitely worth summarizing again here. An A lender is one who specializes in qualified applicants. That is, applicants with solid credit and income confirmation. It's the A lenders where you will find the most favourable interest rates since they are dealing with the most solid, qualified applicants.

A B lender, also sometimes referred to as an equity lender, specializes in working with applicants that won't get approved through an A lender. A lenders qualify their applicants based on credit and income. B lenders qualify more so on the specific property and it's available equity, or size of the down payment if it's a purchase.

B lenders qualify more so on the specific property and it's available equity, or size of the down payment if it's a purchase.

As there is more risk to the lender with these types of transactions, a higher down payment is required. Where you can purchase with as little as 5% down through an A lender, a B lender will require a minimum of 15-20%, however it's not that cut and dry. While they are qualifying more so on the property as opposed to the borrower, they're also going to look at income and credit. Some sort of documented proof of income will be required…. regardless of how much equity or how big your down payment is. The mortgage rate, minimum down payment, and whether or not the mortgage will even be approved will vary depending on any of the following three things:

- Type of property
- Credit
- Location

Type of Property

Is it a house or a condo? Condos are not quite as sought after as houses, therefore condos will typically require a higher down payment.

Credit

While B lenders are a little more lenient with your credit bureau than an A lender would be, they still scrutinize it. However, it's more or less used as a barometer to set your rate and maximum Loan to Value (LTV) as opposed to qualification. For example, someone with a credit score of 495 would require a higher down payment and be quoted a higher rate than someone with a score of 595. Every situation is a little different.

Location

Properties located in urban areas are always easier to finance than properties located in rural communities. Where you'll need a minimum of 15-20% to purchase a property in Mississauga, that same property may require a 35% down payment if located in Belleville for example. Down payment and rate can even vary within a major urban centre if the property is located in a less desirable neighborhood. Certain parts of Toronto and Hamilton for example require a higher down payment, not to mention, a higher rate as well. There are also some locations where these lenders will not lend, regardless of how much money you have to put down.

Rates are also quite a bit higher with B lenders. In most cases, anywhere from 1.50% to 3.50% higher than what an A lender would charge.

Even B lenders have their limits and there are many situations where an applicant still may not qualify. For these applicants, the only option would be with a private lender.

PRIVATE LENDERS

Another common source of alternative lending is private money. Private money typically comes from an individual as opposed to an institution. For example, instead of your lender being RBC, it would be 'Joe Smith'. These are people who have typically done quite well for themselves who are looking for investment opportunities, and in this case, that opportunity lies in alternative mortgage lending.

Another source of private money would be what's known as a Mortgage Investment Corporation, more commonly referred to as a MIC. A MIC is where investor money is pooled together with other investors and then lent out as mortgages.

Where rates with B lenders are about 1.5% to 3.5% more than what a typical A lender would charge, a private lender can be more like 4.5% to 6% higher on a first mortgage. On second mortgages, rates are usually into the double digits with rates typically being in the 10-15% range.

So why would anyone want to pay such a high rate on their mortgage?

The quick answer is that they don't. But in some cases, there are no other alternatives.

Different private lenders have different criteria for lending. Some will limit their mortgages to 75% LTV, while others will go up to 85%. There are a very small number of private lenders that will entertain lending on second mortgages as high as 90%, however this can be even more costly in both rate and in fees. I'll be discussing fees shortly.

Some private lenders will still require similar documentation to what's required with institutional lenders (A & B), however it's not uncommon to find some who will require substantially less. The biggest question lenders have in these situations is whether the deal makes sense or not.

The biggest question lenders have in these situations is whether the deal makes sense or not.

For example, let's say Jim comes to us looking for a second mortgage. He has a past double bankruptcy, a long list of current collections, and no current source of income. He would like to borrower $100,000 on a second mortgage up to 85% his property value, and is vague about what he will be using the money for.

Lending in this situation does not make a lot of sense. Let's break down this deal bit by bit based on what the lenders will be looking at:

He has brutal credit with a double bankruptcy and a long list of collections following the second bankruptcy. Some people never learn and it doesn't seem as though paying bills is, or ever will be a priority for him.

No source of income. Without any income coming in, the applicant has no capacity to repay this mortgage.

High LTV. Going up to 85% of the homes value on such a risky applicant doesn't leave the lender any cushion in the likely event that he would have to force a power of sale on the borrower's home.

The odds of this mortgage going into default are extremely strong and for all these reasons, there isn't a single private lender who would consider lending in this situation. Not any sane one that is. The deal doesn't make any sense and would be a recipe for disaster for all parties involved.

This is an extreme example to illustrate my point.

Now let's take a look at a situation that makes a bit more sense.

Joe just finished going through a messy divorce, which has completely destroyed his credit. He has a bunch of credit card debt, all accumulated from his legal battles with his ex. He's frustrated and would like to get all this behind him so he can start rebuilding his credit. He comes to us looking for a 2nd mortgage of $50,000 which will pay out all his creditors and will also leave some money for some small renovations. He has a salaried government job where he has worked for the past 10 years and has an annual income of $85,000 per year. His home is located in a popular suburb of Toronto with a market value of $600,000 and currently owes $250,000 on his mortgage.

Here are the strong points of this deal:

Since Joe has decent, salaried income with a long history at the same job, it's a safe bet to say that his income will be stable for the foreseeable future. The fact that he has a government job solidifies it even further.

He's borrowing a reasonable amount and has a clear and understandable reason for borrowing the funds.

As the total of his first and new second mortgage will only come to $300,000 on a home that was appraised for $600,000, the LTV is only 50%. There is plenty of equity left in the home, which gives the lender lots of protection should the borrower default on the payments.

He has a great explanation for why he is in this situation to begin with.

Everything about this deal makes sense, so a private lender would have no problem lending him the money he needs.

Just as the first example is an extreme case of a deal that doesn't make sense, this is an extreme case of a deal that does. Private mortgages can be put together for all types of situations, providing they make sense.

*The most important component
in approval of a private mortgage
is the amount of equity in the home.*

The most important component in approval of a private mortgage is the amount of equity in the home. Even the applicant used in the first example above could potentially qualify for a private mortgage if he had enough equity and everything made sense.

What?

How could that situation possibly make any sense?

For this example, we'll use the same applicant with the past double bankruptcy, long list of collections, but we will change some details on the property. Let's say he inherited this property from his parents and had been living in the home for the past 10 years. The property has a market value of $500,000 located in a popular, urban neighborhood, and is owned free and clear. No money owing on it at all. He needs to borrow $100,000 on a 1 year term and the money is going to be used for renovations on the home. While he doesn't have any money to repay the loan, he will take out enough funds to cover the mortgage payments for the year. His plan is to fix up the home and then sell it in a year's time.

Here's how we would look at this situation considering the revised details:

The LTV is only 20% considering he doesn't owe anything on the house right now. ($100,000 divided by $500,000 = 20%).

While he doesn't have any income to support the payments, there will be enough money from the proceeds to ensure the loan gets paid. Considering there is no income and the client has a history of not paying his bills, we would likely deduct the year's payments from the mortgage advance. So if the monthly payment on this mortgage is $1,000, we would deduct $12,000 from the advance of funds. He would be given $88,000 (less fees) on closing with no need to make any additional payments over the year since they have already been covered.

His reasoning for the mortgage makes sense. He has a clear and concise purpose for the money, and he has a solid exit strategy, as his plan is to sell the home once the renovations are complete.

Given the above, this deal is now starting to make a lot more sense and is something I could likely get approved for this applicant.

EXIT STRATEGY

Since alternative lending can get pretty expensive, you're not going to want to be in these types of mortgages forever. Both B lenders and private lenders are meant to be short-term solutions, which is why the terms are usually limited to 1 or 2 years. In situations where my clients require alternative lending due to poor credit, I'll take the time with them to help them rebuild their credit over the term so they will be ready to refinance into a much better mortgage by the time they reach their maturity date.

With all alternative lenders, the key word here is 'marketability'. It all comes down to risk. More equity in the property means less risk.

You can gain access to alternative lenders through a mortgage broker. Most brokers however don't have a lot of sources for private money mortgages, which is an area that we specialize in at CityCan Financial.

FEES ON PRIVATE MORTGAGES

While mortgages from A lenders don't have any set up fees charged by the broker, there would always be fees associated with private lenders. The fee can vary depending on the size of the mortgage, as well as by the particulars of each individual situation. Fees on a first mortgage could be anywhere from 1 – 3% where fees on a second mortgage could be 5-10%. Often private mortgages will also have an additional fee charged by the lender, which can be another 1 – 3%, depending on the situation. On seconds going up to 90% LTV, it would not be uncommon to see a 10% broker fee and a 10% lender fee.

IS IT WORTH IT?

There is no question getting a private mortgage can be pricey. Whether they are actually worth the money or not comes down to the specific situation. There are some cases where people really need the money and have no other alternatives. It can help save their home from power of sale, or can get them needed funds quickly. While expensive, private money can provide a much needed bail out of a sticky situation. When you desperately need money and everyone you talk to slams the door on you, the availability of private money can be a breath of fresh air.

In some cases, it can be purely for investment purposes. Let's say Dave Smith is looking at purchasing a property that is in need of some TLC. His plan is to renovate the property and then flip it for a profit. Dave estimates he will make $100,000 in profit after all his renovation expenses are paid. The problem is, no one will lend him the money. He contacts a broker that quotes him 8% on a private first mortgage of $250,000, with legal, broker and lender fees amounting to $10,000. Dave conservatively estimates the renovations will take about a year to complete. So at the end of the year, he will have paid $20,000 in interest and $10,000 in total fees. Since he'll be making $100,000 from this flip, he'll come out with a profit of $70,000. Considering no one else would lend him the money, the private mortgage allowed him to make $70,000 that he would have had to otherwise pass on. In this case, I would take that action any day of the week.

PRIVATE FIRST AND SECOND MORTGAGES

While private lenders will lend on both first and second mortgages, they are most commonly used for seconds. Since B lenders don't offer second mortgages, private lenders are the only option.

So what is the difference between a first and second mortgage? The terms 'first' and 'second' mortgage refers to the mortgages priority. In other words, if you take a property that is free and clear from any financing, and register a mortgage on it, that mortgage would become a first mortgage. It's a first because there are no other charges (mortgages) against the property, so it's the first to register. If you wanted to put another mortgage on the property at a later date without discharging the first mortgage, then the new mortgage would be considered a second mortgage. This is simply because it's the second mortgage placed on the property. The priority of a mortgage is determined solely by the date in which it was registered. If you were to discharge the first mortgage by paying it out in its entirety, then the second mortgage would become the first, since it would be the only charge on title. There is no longer another mortgage for it to go behind. If you had two mortgages registered on the property and if you were to refinance the first mortgage, then this would require the current first to be discharged and the new mortgage registered. As this new mortgage would be registered at a later date then the registration date on the current second, then the new mortgage would be in second place (second mortgage) and the current second would become the first mortgage since it was registered first.

Since no lender currently holding a first mortgage would accept being behind another lender, meaning they wouldn't accept being in second position, then this is not something that would be allowed. In this case, the current second mortgage lender would need to 'postpone' their registration. This would allow the new mortgage being registered to take priority as the new first mortgage. The current second mortgage would then maintain its position in second place.

In other words, mortgage priority goes by date. If you purchase a home that closes on April 1st, and then need to borrow additional funds on April 30ᵗʰ while leaving your current mortgage intact, then the new mortgage would automatically become a second mortgage.

THE COST OF BAD CREDIT

Having bad credit can cost you thousands of dollars in the mortgage world. I've mentioned that mortgages with B lenders can be as much as 1.5%-3% higher than mortgage rates from an A lender. On a $300,000 mortgage, this can translate into an additional cost of $4,400-$8,900 <u>per year</u>. If you needed to borrow private money, then the additional cost would be significantly higher.

Bad credit is expensive. Period. Sure there are many cases where there is a good explanation for the bad credit. Likely due to an unforeseen and unfortunate event life tossed your way. However there are also many times when the bad credit can be preventable.

Late Payments

While it seems obvious, I can't stress enough how important it is to make your payments on time. Even if the minimum payment on your credit card is $10, make sure you pay that $10 by the due date. Being even one day late with your payment can cause your credit bureau to show a delinquency. It does not distinguish between 1 day late and 30 days late. Late is late. It works in 30 day increments, so your credit gets progressively worse when you hit 31 days, 61 days, 91 days etc, without making a payment.

Even if you miss your minimum payment one month, but pay the entire balance the next month, your credit bureau will still report that a payment was late. The creditor does not care if you pay the entire debt off or not. Honestly, it's in their best interest that you don't! All they care about is that you make your payments on time, as agreed. Set up an automatic payment system if you need to. Many online banking platforms will allow you to do this. Just make sure you make your payments on time.

Going Over Your Limit

Going over your credit limit will also negatively affect your score. Just because you have a $5,000 limit on your credit card doesn't necessarily mean that the creditor won't let you charge $6,000. While they may let the charges go though, your score will be negatively affected as a result. To the credit reporting agency (Equifax, Transunion, etc), you've exceeded your limit, which demonstrates irresponsibility with credit usage.

To keep your credit strong, it's best to stay within 75% of your limit…and don't go over. If you need more, you can always call the credit card company and ask them for a limit increase. A higher limit won't affect you negatively, but going over your limit will.

NO CREDIT

There are some people that prefer not to have any credit at all. They prefer to pay cash and don't want to have the burden of having to make credit card payments. In some cases, they may not trust themselves with having credit cards, so for that reason, they operate by paying cash for everything.

The problem with this is that no credit is equivalent to bad credit in the lending world. There is no evidence as to whether you'll make your payments on time… or at all.

> ### *No credit is equivalent to*
> ### *bad credit in the lending world.*

Even the B lenders put up their guard and tighten their approval process for someone without a credit score. In fact, they would rather see bad credit than no credit in many cases. At least then they have an idea and can accurately assess their risk. When there has been no past demonstration of credit responsibility, B lenders will still lend to you, however they'll require a higher down payment and will likely quote a higher rate than what would have been given if there were a credit score reporting.

HOW TO REPAIR YOUR CREDIT

Repairing bad credit is not a difficult process, it just takes some time and it's not going to happen overnight. It can be as simple as ensuring that you're not late on any payments. You don't have to pay off all your debt, but just make sure you start making your payments on time. If you are in arrears on any loans, make sure these are brought up to date. If you are over your limit on any of your accounts, then you need to bring your balance down below the limit. Ideally, below 75% of the limit. Below 50% is even better when you are in the rebuilding phase.

Make sure you keep your credit accounts open. If you feel you have an excessive amount of available credit and would prefer to close some, then start with the accounts that are more recent and keep the ones you have had for longer. The longer you have had a credit card, the stronger it makes your credit bureau. You'll want to keep at least two of the older accounts open.

Any collections reporting on your credit bureau will need to be addressed. If you don't agree with the collection, or think it's there in error, then you need to contact the creditor to work something out with them. The longer you leave it the harder it will be to fix. While your score will still repair itself with active collections, any mortgage lender will require them to be paid out or settled before they will approve you for a mortgage.

If you've declared bankruptcy, entered into a consumer proposal, or if you don't have any active credit, then the only way to get on the road to credit recovery is to get some new credit.

Secured Credit Cards

Sure, no one will approve you for a credit card due to your history, which is why you'll need to start off with a secured credit card. A secured credit card is where you prepay the limit amount, so the credit issuer doesn't have to worry about non-payment. For example, you pay $500 to the credit card issuer, at which point, they send you a credit card with a $500 limit. The card is secured by the $500. You then use it just like any other credit card. The creditor will send you a statement at the end of the month showing your balance and minimum payment due. You can either pay it off or just make the minimum payment. If you decide to carry a balance on the card, you'll pay interest on that amount….just like with a regular credit card. Your activity on this card then gets reported to your credit bureau, and voila!

You now have active credit!

Just as I mentioned above, don't be even slightly late on any of the payments and ensure you don't go over your limit. This can be particularly detrimental when you are in the rebuilding stage.

Once you have had your secured card for a few months, ask them if they can convert it to an unsecured card. If they say no, wait a few more months and then try again. Once they've agreed, you'll then want to apply for another unsecured card. If you are declined for the unsecured card then wait another 6 months and try again.

Capital One and Home Trust are both institutions offering secured credit cards. Most major banks offer them as well. When applying, make sure it is in fact a secured credit card and not a Visa or Mastercard debit card, as they won't do anything for your credit.

As with any credit card, you want to ensure you're using it responsibly. Having new credit shouldn't give you an excuse to spend more money.

Use your credit wisely.

> *Having new credit shouldn't give you an excuse to spend more money.*

QUALIFYING FOR A MORTGAGE WITH REBUILT CREDIT

To qualify for a decent mortgage rate, you'll ideally want to have two active trade lines, preferably both revolving such as a credit card or a line of credit. Each revolving account (credit card, line of credit, etc) should have a minimum credit limit of $1,500. Preferably higher. Having a higher limit demonstrates stronger credit responsibility. If your limits are lower than this, you'll want to ask for an increase. For strong credit, each trade line should have a full one year history. Some lenders even require two.

Sometimes exceptions can be made if the amount of available credit falls a little short, but you may be somewhat limited in options. Some lenders can be real sticklers for borrowers to meet these minimum credit requirements.

CHAPTER EIGHT HIGHLIGHTS

- If you have damaged credit, you still may qualify for a mortgage through an alternative lender. A <u>minimum</u> down payment / equity position of 15% is typically required for it to even be considered.
- Alternative lending can get quite expensive, so they are meant to be short-term solutions.
- A second mortgage is usually offered at a higher rate than a first mortgage.
- Bad credit can get extremely expensive. Always ensure you pay all your bills on time and stay within your credit limit.
- Try to maintain at least two credit cards, each with a minimum limit of $1,500 to ensure strong, healthy credit.

- No credit is equal to bad credit.
- You can start to repair bad credit with a secured credit card.

Life is full of ups and downs, and while we try to maintain solid credit, it can be tough when life decides to deal you a bad hand. While expensive, alternative lending can be a lifesaver for many. Quite often however, bad credit can be avoided. Believe me, life is a lot more fun when you don't have to worry about paying thousands of dollars in unnecessary expenses per year. Just think of all the fun things you could be doing with that money you are throwing away.

CONCLUSION

THERE IS NO DOUBT THE mortgage world can be confusing. Really, you're at the mercy of whom you're dealing with, particularly if you don't take the time to shop around and talk to different banks and brokers. The biggest mistake one can make is to walk into their bank and give them your mortgage business without doing any research, or without asking them any questions about their experience level. Just because someone is sitting behind a desk with a bright and shiny bank logo on their business card, it does not necessarily make them a knowledgeable and trustworthy individual. Just as dealing with a licensed mortgage agent doesn't necessarily make them a knowledgeable and trustworthy individual.

By having a much stronger sense of how mortgages work, you can contact your bank or broker armed with knowledge, giving you the upper hand in beating the bank at their own game.

Knowledge is power!

With the right knowledge, you can likely save thousands of dollars over the term of your mortgage, but you of course have to act on what you've learned. To know but not act is to not know at all. Knowledge is useless without action.

You now have a game plan.

The past 8 chapters will give you a significant advantage when shopping for your next mortgage and you'll have a better understanding than the vast majority of Canadian borrowers. You now know that there are other options and that there is opportunity to potentially save thousands over what you may have been paying in the past. You now possess strategies to increase your savings even further.

The information in this book will also come in handy when you come to me looking for your next mortgage! Please check out my website at www.easy123mortgage.ca for all the latest information. I look forward to working with you on your mortgage in the near future.

COMMON MORTGAGE TERMINOLOGY

Amortization

The amount of time it takes to pay a loan down to a zero balance over a fixed period based on equal periodic payments, including accrued interest on the outstanding balance.

Annual percentage rate (A.P.R.)

The APR factors in the full cost of a loan including any associated fees expressed as a yearly percentage rate.

Appraisal

An estimate of the value of property, performed by an accredited appraiser.

Appraised Value

An opinion of a property's fair market value, based on an appraiser's knowledge, experience, and analysis of the property.

Assumability

An assumable mortgage is one that can be transferred from the seller of the home to the new buyer. The new buyer would have to qualify in the same way they would for any other type of mortgage.

Assumption

The agreement between buyer and seller where the buyer takes over the rate and payments on an existing mortgage from the seller. Assuming a mortgage can potentially save the buyer money in an environment where rates have increased since the original arrangement of the mortgage.

Accelerated Biweekly

Dividing your monthly mortgage payment in half and then making that payment every two weeks. The result works out to making the equivalent of one additional monthly payment per year which goes directly to the principal, therefore accelerating the payoff of the mortgage. This will reduce a 25 year amortization down to 22 years, 3 months, saving the borrower a substantial amount of interest.

Basis Points

Basis points (abbreviated as BPS) are fractions of 1%. For example, 1 basis point is equivalent to 0.01%.

Blanket Mortgage

A mortgage registered over at least two pieces of real estate as security for the same mortgage.

Borrower (Mortgagor)

One who applies for and receives a loan in the form of a mortgage with the intention of repaying the loan in full.

Bridge Loan

A loan to cover a borrower for the portion of down payment coming from the sale of their current home where the closing date of the new home falls before the sale of the current home.

Broker (Mortgage)

A licensed professional who brings a borrower and a lender together, but doesn't lend out their own money, nor do they work for the lending institution. A broker represents multiple mortgage lenders and can give the borrower more options over going to the mortgage lender directly.

Cash Flow
The amount of cash left over from rent payments after all expenses have been paid on an income-producing property.

Closing Date
The date in which the real estate transaction is finalized and the property and funds legally change hands.

Closed Mortgage
Any mortgage with restrictions on additional payments made before its maturity. Most mortgages in Canada are closed. This is the opposite of an open mortgage.

CMHC (Canadian Mortgage and Housing Corporation)
One of three organizations in Canada offering mortgage default insurance on high-ratio mortgages.

Closing Costs
Costs such as legal fees, title insurance, land transfer tax, etc, that are incurred when purchasing property and are paid by the borrower on closing date.

Conventional Mortgage
Any mortgage with a loan to value (LTV) ratio of 80% or less (A mortgage with a down payment of 20% or more).

Credit Bureau

A report documenting the credit history and current status of a borrower's credit standing.

Credit Score

A credit score used to determine a borrowers credit worthiness and is comprised of past credit utilization. There are two credit reporting agencies in Canada, Equifax and Transunion.

Debt service ratio

A ratio expressed as a percentage demonstrating your monthly debt obligation in relation to your gross monthly income. There are two debt service ratios used in Canada. The GDS, or Gross Debt Service Ratio, which is your mortgage payment, property tax, heat, and ½ of condo fee (if applicable) divided by your gross income. The other ratio used is the TDS, or Total Debt Service Ratio, which is the same as the GDS calculation, but also factors in other monthly debt obligations. The maximum GDS for qualification is 35% for those with credit scores under 680 or 39% for those with scores over 680. The TDS will allow up to 42% and 44% respectively.

Default

Failure to make the scheduled payments on a mortgage.

Delinquency

Failure to make payments on time, which can be either your mortgage payment or any other monthly debt obligation reporting on your credit bureau.

Down Payment

A percentage of the purchase price required for a borrower to pay on or before closing date when purchasing real estate. The minimum down payment required is 5%.

Equity

The difference between the fair market value and current debt secured against the property.

First Mortgage

The primary lien against a property.

Fixed Rate Mortgage

The mortgage interest rate is locked in throughout the term of the mortgage.

GDS

(see Gross Debt Service Ratio)

Genworth Financial

One of three organizations in Canada offering mortgage default insurance on high-ratio mortgages.

Gross Debt Service Ratio (GDS)

The annual charges for principal, interest, taxes and heat divided by the annual gross household income. This can also be determined on a monthly basis. The maximum GDS ratio for mortgage qualification is 35% for clients with credit scores under 680 and 39% for those with scores of 680 and above. The GDS ratio along with the TDS ratio (total debt service ratio) are used together to determine mortgage qualification on income.

Hard Money
A term more commonly used in the United States which is another name for private money, which is the term typically used in Canada.

HELOC
A Home Equity Line of Credit is exactly as the name implies. It's a line of credit secured against the equity in your home.

High Ratio Mortgage
Any mortgage in Canada with a loan to value (LTV) higher than 80% requiring mortgage default insurance. For example, a mortgage with less than 20% down payment. The opposite of this would be a conventional mortgage, which would have 20% or greater down payment.

Interest Only Mortgage
A loan where the payments cover only the interest and no principal is paid down. These mortgages are typically 1 year terms. As there is no principal being paid back, there is no amortization period. Interest Only mortgages are primarily given through private mortgage lenders.

Installment
The scheduled mortgage payment that a borrower agrees to make to a lender.

Interest
The cost associated with borrowing money.

Liabilities
A person's financial obligations, which include both long term and short term debt.

Lien
A claim against a piece of property for the payment or satisfaction of a debt.

Loan-to-Value Ratio (LTV)
The relationship between the amount of the mortgage loan and the appraised value of the property expressed as a percentage

Market Value
The highest price that a buyer would pay and the lowest price a seller would accept on a property.

Maturity Date
The date in which the principal balance of a mortgage becomes due and payable. The mortgage could then be paid off in full, renewed, or switched to a different lender.

Monthly Fixed Installment
The principal and interest portion of a mortgage payment.

Mortgage
A legal document that offers a property to the lender as security for payment of a debt.

Mortgage Broker
An individual or a company who arranges mortgages with multiple lenders. This is a free service for qualified borrowers.

The mortgage specialist at the bank is not a broker as they only arrange mortgages through the bank they work for.

Mortgage Term
The length of time for which the money is borrowed. The most common mortgage term is 5 years, but can also be 6 months, 1, 2, 3, 4, 5, 6, 7 or 10 years. Not to be confused with amortization.

Mortgagee
The lender.

Mortgage Default Insurance
Insurance that protects the lender should the borrower default on the mortgage loan. This is what allows a borrower to purchase a home with less than 20% down payment.

Mortgage Life Insurance
A type of term life insurance. In the event that the borrower dies while the policy is in force, the debt is automatically paid by the insurance proceeds.

Mortgagor
The borrower or homeowner.

Negative Amortization
When the fixed payment does not include any amount for principal reduction and doesn't cover all of the interest. The mortgage balance therefore increases instead of decreasing.

Negative Cash Flow
When operating expenses on a rental property are greater than the rental income.

Net Operating Income (NOI)

Income produced by a property after deducting all operating expenses (not including mortgage payments) from the gross rental income produced by the property. Cash flow is determined by subtracting mortgage payments from the NOI.

Open Mortgage

This allows the borrower to make additional payments of any amount, or pay off the entire mortgage at any time without penalty.

Power of Sale

When the lender forces the sale where they have been unsuccessful in collecting on defaulted payments by the borrower.

Private Money

Money lent by private individuals to borrowers who don't qualify through traditional lending sources.

Rate Hold Period

A lender's guarantee that the mortgage rate quoted will be good for a specific number of days from date of application.

Trade Line

A credit card, line of credit, or any type of loan that appears on your credit bureau.

ABOUT THE AUTHOR

AFTER HAVING MULTIPLE BAD EXPERIENCES going through the mortgage application process, Paul figured there had to be a better way. People deserved to have better treatment, better service, and more overall respect from professionals arranging their mortgage. He decided to take things into his own hands by entering the mortgage business in 2007, and since then, he has never looked back. He strives to ensure clients needs are attended to promptly with strong communication through the entire process, and has built a solid reputation as an expert in his field.

Paul currently resides downtown Toronto where spending quality time with his friends and family is something that is extremely important to him. In his spare time, whenever he can find it, he enjoys reading, writing, downhill skiing and snowmobiling, however his biggest passion is boating.

CONTACT INFO

Get in touch for all of your mortgage needs.
www.easy123mortgage.ca
paulm@citycan.com
416-409-8009
twitter.com/paulmeredith
facebook.com/mortgagebrokertoronto
linkedin.com/in/paul-meredith-ontario-mortgages-317578a